**Hobbies Through Children's
Books and Activities**

HOBBIES THROUGH CHILDREN'S BOOKS AND ACTIVITIES

Nancy Allen Jurenka

2001
TEACHER IDEAS PRESS
Libraries Unlimited
A Division of Greenwood Publishing Group, Inc.
Englewood, Colorado

*"There is always one moment in childhood
when the door opens and lets the future in."*

Graham Greene, *The Power and the Glory*
(New York: Viking, 1940)

Copyright © 2001 Nancy Allen Jurenka
All Rights Reserved
Printed in the United States of America

No part of this publication may be reproduced, stored in a retrieval system, or transmitted, in any form or by any means, electronic, mechanical, photocopying, recording, or otherwise, without the prior written permission of the publisher. An exception is made for individual librarians and educators, who may make copies of activity sheets for classroom use in a single school or library. Standard citation information should appear on each page.

TEACHER IDEAS PRESS
Libraries Unlimited
A Division of Greenwood Publishing Group, Inc.
P.O. Box 6633
Englewood, CO 80155-6633
1-800-237-6124
www.lu.com/tip

Library of Congress Cataloging-in-Publication Data

Jurenka, Nancy Allen, 1937-
    Hobbies through children's books and activities / Nancy Allen Jurenka.
      p. cm.
    Includes bibliographical references and index.
    ISBN 1-56308-773-1 (pbk.)
     1. Hobbies. 2. Hobbies -- Juvenile literature -- Bibliography. 3. Activity programs in education. I. Title.

GV1201 .J87 2001
790.1'3'083--dc21
                                                   2001027624

P

> In order to keep this title in print and available to the academic community, this edition was produced using digital reprint technology in a relatively short print run. This would not have been attainable using traditional methods. Although the cover has been changed from its original appearance, the text remains the same and all materials and methods used still conform to the highest book-making standards.

CONTENTS

Acknowledgments vii

Introduction ix

1—Architecture 1

2—Birds 7

3—Cats 13

4—Dancing 17

5—Dogs 21

6—Drawing and Painting 27

7—Egg Decoration 31

8—Face Painting 35

9—Fishing 39

10—Horses 43

11—Insects 47

12— Jewelry Making 53

13—Kites 59

14—Mask Construction 65

15—Music 71

16—Pottery 75

17—Puppets 79

18—Puzzles and Games 83

19—Quilts 89

20—Rock Collecting 95

21—Scrapbook Construction 101

22—Show Biz 107

23—Stamp Collecting 111

24—Stars 115

25—Starting a Business 119

26—Storytelling 127

27—Teddy Bears 135

28—Toys 141

29—Trains 147

30—Weaving 153

Activities Index 161

Author/Title/Subject Index 163

About the Author 169

ACKNOWLEDGMENTS

Hobbies Through Children's Books and Activities resulted from information gathered from many people. Central Washington University colleagues and students, as well as friends, provided me with much-appreciated advice and information. The librarians at the King County Library in Bellevue, Washington were most helpful as were those in Corvallis, Oregon and Yakima, Washington. Erin Sprague, the editor for this book, deserves much appreciation for her advice and guidance. Thank you, all of you.

INTRODUCTION

The purpose of this book is to promote literacy and a lifelong interest in reading through connecting books to children's hobbies. A special emphasis is placed on informational (nonfiction) books. But first, children must be introduced to and encouraged to acquire hobbies. Therefore, directions are given for little appetizers (hobby starters) for thirty children's hobbies. Having whetted their appetites for a hobby, boys and girls are encouraged to read more about it in informational, how-to books.

It is important for adults in children's lives to bring children along the paths in life. Therefore, this book is written for use by the adults in children's lives, most importantly, parents, as well as leaders of 4-H clubs, boys clubs, and scout troops; parents of home-schooled children; teachers; children's museum personnel; after-school caretakers; literacy program volunteers; social workers; and mentors.

This book is written to provide adults in children's lives with clues about children's interests in hobbies and hobby-related books, to increase children's vocabulary, and to introduce them to hobby-related poetry, as well as other language development activities.

THE BENEFITS OF HOBBIES

Having a hobby is a great gift. It brings much joy and satisfaction to our lives. Some hobbies, such as stamp collecting, can be enjoyed alone yet shared with others who have a mutual interest. Hobbies can provide a respite from the demands and emotional pressures of school, competition, and work.

- A hobby is a passion that may (not must) be pursued just for the love of it. Children who have a hobby see themselves as capable. No boss or teacher stands over us demanding that we meet someone else's standards. It is an activity done because we want to, not because we have to. What a relief that is!

- A hobby is a way to give expression to our interests. We are naturally curious. We want to find out. There comes that moment when some thing, sound, movement, or sight draws us in. Something takes our breath away, rivets our attention. Our curiosity becomes aroused, and our imagination begins to spin. Our senses are stimulated beyond the ordinary reaction, and we become passionate about it. It could be the determination to play a trumpet, earn the affection of a cat, find a unique stamp, or finally perceive the outline of a constellation.

- A hobby frees us from boredom in a worthwhile way. As humans, we hate being bored. Our mental makeup often seems to have one mission: to find something to do that is totally absorbing.

- Unfortunately, too many of us spend our recreational time parked in front of a television or computer screen. Not only may television promote violence, but it also keeps us from communicating with those around us and engaging in more active pastimes. Every April, the United States marks National TV-Turnoff Week. According to Barbara Cornell's article "Pulling the Plug on TV," the consequences, as measured by Barbara Brock, a researcher from Eastern Washington University, are admirable. Turning off the television improves literacy. Brock discovered that four-fifths of children in TV-free households had above-average reading skills. When families encourage TV-free time, they involve themselves in activities that bring them closer to each other. The number of minutes spent conversing with family members increases significantly. Hobbies are great alternatives to watching television or playing computer games, and they provide parents with opportunities to connect with their children.

- Instead of staring passively, glaze-eyed in front of a flickering cathode tube, we are actively creating, collecting, making, and doing something worthwhile. That something may be tap dancing, lacing pony beads into a zipper pull, leading younger children in games, collecting teddy bears, or providing a dog walking service to neighbors.

- A childhood hobby has the potential to become a career or profession. So often, famous people make mention that they became passionate about their career during some childhood incident that sparked in them an enthusiasm that lasts a lifetime. For example, Oprah Winfrey often mentions her early childhood interest in public speaking.

- A hobby can be a respite from the demands of a stress-filled profession. Franklin Delano Roosevelt spoke of the solace he felt when he was occupied with his stamp collection. Frank Sinatra looked forward to the time he could spend with his extensive model train collection.

- A hobby is a bridge to the wider community. A person with a hobby is a person with something to give, to share, with others. Nearly all hobbies have local, regional, and national organizations. Magicians meet with other magicians, stargazers gather on mountaintops, puppeteers have conventions, and dog lovers have dog shows. Communities are enriched because hobbyists are willing to share their interests by speaking at schools, youth groups, and retirement homes. Hobbyists provide a welcome service to the community.

- Sharing a hobby helps an individual become part of a community. If you are a father who has taught your daughter how to construct a kite, you have increased the possibility for the two of you to engage the other children in your apartment building or neighborhood with this activity. In this manner, a hobby becomes a coin that may be used to create social capital.

Much has been reported about the disintegration of our society, the breakdown of the family, and the adverse effects that this situation has on the individual and the community. In the words of Robert Putnam, we have lost our social capital. In Robert Putnam's book, *Bowling Alone*, he tells us that the important indicators of a nation's social strength (e.g., civic participation, church attendance, club membership) show that the number of people involved in these activities, which glue society together, has decreased drastically. It seems that we are living increasingly isolated lives. This situation is neither healthy for the individual, nor for the community.

- Sharing a hobby with like-minded people increases our feelings of well-being, gives us warm feelings of camaraderie, and increases our self-esteem. When the members of a hobby-related group do an about-face and turn their talent, energy, and good will toward others in the wider community, social capital is increased. An example of one such group is Quilts from Caring Hands. These Oregon hobbyists create tactile quilts and toys for visually impaired children. In addition, they construct pre-Braille activity books for preschool children.

- Hobbies connect children to many cultures. When children string beads, create Ukrainian Easter eggs, or construct toys, they are participating in activities shared by children around the world.

Our intellectual, social, emotional, mental, and physical health is greatly improved as we participate actively in our hobbies, our passionate interests.

BRINGING A CHILD ALONG

As grown-ups in a group with children, we find that we are being watched. Children look to us to share our skills, interests, and talents with them. Whether we are Mom creating a beaded bracelet at the kitchen table, Dad tinkering under the hood of the car, an older brother practicing magic tricks, or a big sister organizing the neighborhood kids to put on a play, we look around and meet the curiosity and "help me do that" in a child's eyes. So bring a child along the paths of life; help a child develop a hobby.

You might be saying to yourself, "I don't have a hobby to share." Think again. Can you remember a time when you were a child constructing or creating something along with your friends or family members? When I told people that I was writing this book, they told me stories. One woman, who is now a successful artist, remembered that when she was a child, her mother rolled out lengths of butcher paper on the dining room table. She gave the children scissors and glue along with a collection of scraps of magazines, fabric, and cardboard and told them to have fun making collages. Another woman remembered a time when she was six and her mother taught her to knit, a hobby she enjoys to this day. Not only are hobbies happy memory makers, they are also activities that we may pass along to children.

And remember, you do not need to possess the skill of Martha Stewart to introduce a hobby to boys and girls. Enjoy learning together. That's one of the reasons for this book. Hobbies need to be shared one person with another, and the books cited here are the bridges. Borrow children's hobby books from the library. You don't have to be an expert to share a hobby.

FAMILY AND GROUP GLUE

Hobby development has the potential to bring family and group members closer to each other. As adults and children work together on a hobby project, good things start to happen. Authentic conversations and communication begin. The people in the group are focused on the activity that they have in common. Solidarity among group and family members begins to grow. Cooperation rather than competition is emphasized. For this child-friendly atmosphere to occur, it is important to accentuate the positive and forget the negative. Create a climate of admiration. Establish a "put-down free zone."

Sometimes the most difficult behavior for many adults to give up is criticism. We need to eliminate from our vocabulary the words *not*, *don't*, and *can't*. Instead, we need to make it a habit to observe a child's behavior, and as soon as the child has done the right thing, say so by identifying it. This behavior is especially important during any hesitant first steps.

"You threw the ball to the correct spot above your head!" or "Good! You held your arms at waist level." are examples of targeted, positive communication. We adults need to make it a habit to praise and support children in a positive manner.

In addition to setting the right climate for interests to germinate and skills to improve, materials must be available to children. If the stuff is accessible, children will use it. As much as possible, have the following materials and tools on hand and ready to go:

Woven (not knitted) fabric scraps	Wheat paste
Thread	White glue
Cord	Wooden dowels
Large-eyed needles	Large appliance cartons
Papers	Duplicating paper cartons
Fabric glue	Old towels
Fabric paint	Water-based clay
Scissors	Varnish
Pinking shears	Shellac
Modeling clay	Index cards
Carton knife	Balls of various sizes
Fusible fabric	Sidewalk chalk
Foam board	Jigsaw puzzles
Cardboard	Canceled stamps

Tagboard	Cooking equipment
Papier-mâché	Flannel
Crayons	Felt
Markers	Cylindrical oatmeal cartons
Tempera paint	Brads
Paintbrushes	Rubber stamps
Newspaper	Empty thread spools
Nuts	Clean Styrofoam trays
Bolts	String
Screws	Yarn
Springs	Fiber (suitable for weaving)
Stapler	Cardboard tubing
Tape	Clean, empty milk cartons
Egg cartons	Plastic soda bottles
Margarine tubs	Mesh onion bags
Pencils	Birdseed
Compass	Newsprint paper
Batteries	Terra-cotta flowerpots
Copper wire	Pony beads
Balsa wood	Garbage bags
Water-based, nontoxic face paint or makeup	

With this combination of a willingness to learn together, a lot of books, a positive, supportive atmosphere, targeted praise, and plenty of accessible materials, we are on our way to encouraging the growth and development of a lifelong interest in hobbies. When we connect the hobby with reading hobby-related books, we are also in a good position to develop a child's literacy skills.

READING IS EXPERIENCE-BASED

The whole point of reading is to comprehend what the author is stating in written language. Reading is experience-based. The reading process is an interaction between the reader's experience and the author's. The closer the reader's experience is with the author's, the higher the rate of comprehension.

The hands-on experiences provided by a hobby (e.g., gardening) become the basic building blocks for thinking, comprehension, vocabulary development, and authentic understanding of written language.

Hobbies provide dozens of hands-on experiences that in turn connect to language: speaking, listening, writing, and reading. For example, a parent or an adult leader and children may experience the fun and silliness of face painting. As the activity is going on, there will be a lot of chatter and laughter. After experimenting and just having fun, the parent or leader may choose to take the group to the library to find children's books about face painting in order to read more about it.

START A HOBBY, GROW VOCABULARY

Every hobby has a specialized vocabulary associated with it. For example, if a child acquires an interest in fishing, she may naturally acquire new concepts and words, such as creel, pectoral fin, or piscatorial. This situation provides those in the know with an opportunity to help children expand their vocabulary. Expecting children to use hobby-related words in their writing and everyday conversations, as well as to comprehend hobby-related words when encountering them in reading, results in an increase in the children's vocabularies. In *Teaching Children to Read*, D. Ray Reutzel and Robert B. Cooter Jr. state, "Vocabulary is learned best through direct hands on experiences."

THE ORGANIZATION OF THE BOOK

Hobbies Through Children's Books and Activities contains thirty hobby-related lessons. By providing boys and girls with these lessons, you will be introducing them to a life enriched by a passionate interest in a hobby, hobby-related books, and improved literacy.

Each lesson consists of:

- An introduction
- A picture book description
- A starter activity
- A language arts activity
- A poetry suggestion
- Vocabulary words
- References to other resources
- Annotated bibliographies of related books

The Introduction

The introduction discusses the value of the hobby, the skills that may be acquired, and the career possibilities that might come from an interest in that particular hobby.

The Picture Book

The picture book bibliographic reference and annotation gives the parent or leader a door into the hobby. Reading the picture book to the children is a way to introduce the hobby. Each book is coded with the letters (P), (P–I), (I), or (I–A). These are approximate indications of the grade level of the book. (P) is equivalent to the primary grades, K–3. (P–I) indicates grades 2–4. (I) indicates books for grades 4–6, and the (I–A) designation is given to books appropriate for the intermediate through high school grades.

Hobby Starter Activity

The Hobby Starter Activity is a suggested way to introduce the hobby to a group of children. You don't have to be an expert to share a beginner's enthusiasm about a hobby. These activities are intended to be fun and easy. Learn along with the boys and girls in your group. Invite community hobbyists to share their hobbies with your group.

Gather the materials needed for the activity. Encourage children to explore and experiment. From time to time, a limited amount of direct instruction may be needed. It is important, however, not to be heavy-handed. This is a time for fun-in-process, not a perfect product.

Language Arts Activity

The Language Arts Activity extends and enriches the experience with speaking, listening, writing, and reading. The activity cements the connection between involvement with a hobby and language. It gives the children the opportunity to put into words what they have just experienced.

Poem

The poem reference provides the title of a poem related to the hobby. Poetry brings emotional commentary to the activities in which we engage. A poem offers imagery rather than mere description and thus captures a child's imagination. Whimsical, comical, wistful, happy, or sad, the poet's words and cadence enrich our experiences and us.

A trip to the public library will lead you to the *Children's Poetry Index* in which poems are listed by topic. Take the time to locate and share a hobby-related poem. Reading a poem to children adds a grace note that will make the moment magical.

Vocabulary Growth Words

Hobby-related words and their definitions are provided. I suggest that these words be listed with their definitions on poster board or chart paper. Draw the children's attention to them.

If you desire, expand on these words with activities that emphasize relationships among words. Descriptions of a few of these activities follow.

Semantic Webbing

In this activity, graphically portrayed by Dale Johnson and P. David Pearson in *Teaching Reading Vocabulary*, the main concept is placed within a circle on chart paper. Children are asked to call out word associations. Leaders should add their own. The leader will then group the associations into categories as they form. After a category becomes clear and is recorded, it is easier to think of even more associations. A modified semantic web for stamp collecting is shown below.

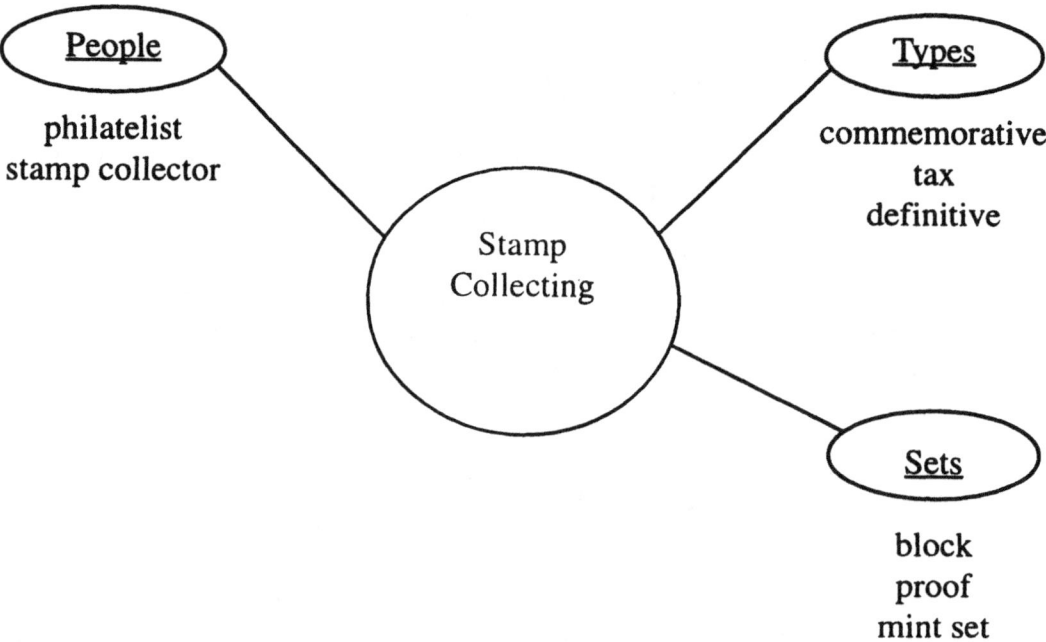

Figure 1. Semantic web.

Feature Analysis

As described by Johnson and Pearson, feature analysis aids children in discovering the similarities and differences among words. The leader writes the topic in the upper left corner of chart paper or of a grid drawn on the board. The leader asks for various types of subsets (words) associated with the topic. These are listed in a column on the far left side of the paper. The leader asks for features associated with each item. Figure 2 is an example of a semantic feature analysis grid using the topic, "Jewelry." If we were in a group together, you might find yourself disagreeing with some of the decisions, and a lively discussion would ensue. Out of the discussion would come clarification and learning.

Jewelry

Types	Features			
	Made with Gemstones	Strung together	Needs findings	Uses gold
Necklace	+	+	−	+
Bracelets	+	+	−	+
Pins	+	−	+	+
Earrings	+	+	+	+
Lanyards	−	−	−	−

Figure 2. Feature analysis chart.

The features are listed across the top of the chart. The leader asks whether or not each feature is associated with the types listed in the far left column. Then the leader writes a plus sign in those blocks in which the feature is associated with an item and a minus sign in those that are not.

As the lesson progresses, a discussion about similarities and differences begins. It is out of this discussion that learning naturally takes place. It becomes useful to expand the grid and to use the letter *S* for *sometimes*.

Venn Diagram

A Venn diagram is a graphic representation showing the comparison between two major ideas or concepts. A discussion is held that elicits what the two have in common and what attributes belong exclusively to one or the other.

For example, a discussion leader may wish to compare "draft horses" with "cutting horses." The resulting Venn diagram might look like this:

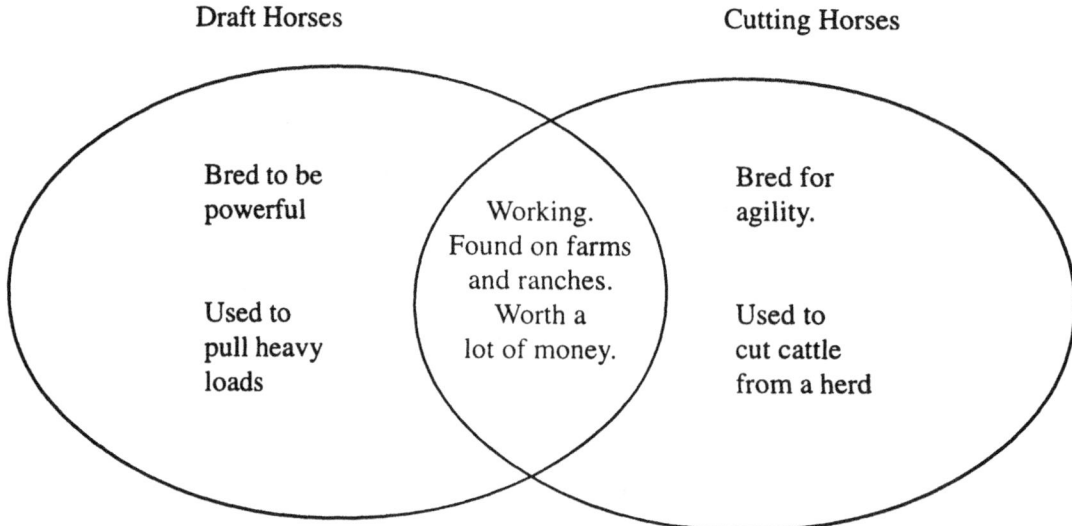

Figure 3. Venn diagram.

Resources

These references are citations of hobby-related museums, Web sites, or associations. Many of the associations have junior divisions that make an effort to help children with their skills and interests in hobbies. Some have Web sites just for children while others provide information about the organization or curricular materials for adults.

Read More About It

At the end of each lesson is an annotated bibliography containing informational books related to the featured hobby. Every attempt was made to include books written in the past decade—ones that likely will be on library shelves. While not all may still be found on bookstore shelves, they are for the most part, still available from the publisher. Online booksellers may be able to locate books that your bookstore or library does not have.

Today's nonfiction books are contemporary informational books that have improved greatly in the past decade. Authors have become more aware of the need to simplify step-by-step directions so that children may follow them independently. Earlier how-to books for children were overwhelming tomes giving far more information than anyone would want to know. Today, illustrations are clear and colorful. Recent books about hobbies attract children to them with graphics and formats, which appeal to visually sophisticated youngsters.

Each book in the Read More About It section is coded with an approximate grade level. (P) refers to books appropriate for the primary grades. (P–I) indicates the book is appropriate for grades 2–4. (I) is used for books appropriate for the intermediate grades (4–6), and (I–A) indicates that the book is appropriate for grade-levels ranging from intermediate through high school.

REFERENCES

Blackburn, G. Meredith III. *Index to Poetry for Children and Young People*. New York: H. W. Wilson.

Cornell, Barbara. "Pulling the Plug on TV." *TIME SELECT/Families* 156, no. 16 (Oct. 16, 2000): F16. Available: http://www.time.com/time/magazine/article/0,9171,91805,00.html.

Johnson, Dale, and P. David Pearson. *Teaching Reading Vocabulary*. New York: Holt, Rinehart and Winston, 1978.

Putnam, Robert D. *Bowling Alone*. New York: Simon & Schuster, 2000.

Reutzel, D. Ray, and Robert B. Cooter Jr. *Teaching Children to Read*. 3d ed. Upper Saddle River, NJ: Prentice Hall, 2000.

1
ARCHITECTURE

The hobby of architecture leads to a multitude of skills, facts, and new words. Taking an interest in the world of building design causes a child to be curious about why things are the way they are, why some proportions are more pleasing than others, and why one building is majestic while another is ugly. An interest in architecture engenders knowledge of various historical styles. Harmony of the parts, scale, goodness of design, varieties of style, line, and shape make up the several qualities that boys and girls may experience through the study of architecture.

The relationship of art to mathematics comes into play as children experiment with designing and constructing buildings born of their imaginations. An interest in history occurs as children investigate the styles characteristic of various historical periods. The architecture of various cultures and countries provides children with a chance to compare and contrast the works of diverse peoples.

New words such as *plinth*, *lintel*, *flying buttress*, *Gothic*, *yurt*, and *domicile* will become part of each child's vocabulary as they play around with the study of architecture.

Historian, construction contractor, urban designer, engineer, graphic designer, architect, art teacher, and theatrical set designer are a few of the careers possible for the child whose eye is caught by a majestic building.

Chorao, Kay. *Cathedral Mouse*. E. P. Dutton, 1988. 32p. Illustrated by Kay Chorao. (P)

Mouse longs for a home. Escaping from a cat, he dashes into an unlikely spot for a home—a vast, echoing cathedral. After exploring various places inside this grand building, he settles down on the top of a pillar. Mysteriously, he is treated every day with cheese and bread until one day he meets his benefactor, a stone carver. The stone carver befriends Mouse and at story's end creates a special home for him.

HOBBY STARTER ACTIVITY

▪ *Build a Castle, Build Your Vocabulary*

Materials

Cereal boxes	Construction paper
Paper towel tubes	String or cord
Toilet paper tubes	Cardboard
Shallow box lid	Match boxes (empty; of various sizes)
Scissors	Foil
Paper (various sizes)	Pictures of castles
Pencils	Pipe cleaners
Poster paint	Nontoxic glue
Corrugated cardboard	Tape
Crayons	Plastic bottles (empty and clean; any size or type)
Milk or juice cartons (paper; empty and clean; of various sizes)	

A well-proportioned castle can be constructed by starting with a gatehouse made from an empty quart milk carton. Pint-size milk cartons can be used to construct the four towers at the corners of the castle grounds. Cardboard may be used to construct the walls (called battlements) that join the towers with the gatehouse and surround the castle grounds.

Assemble the tools, materials, and castle pictures. Have the children use their imaginations to construct the castle. Helpful books are: *Build Your Own Castle* by Kate Petty, published by Franklin Watts; *A Three Dimensional Medieval Castle* by Willabel Tong, published by Viking; *Castles* by Francesca Baines, published by Watts; and *Knights and Castles* by Avery Hart and Paul Mantell, published by Williamson Publishing.

Cutting, pasting, and coloring techniques plus imagination and problem solving will get the job done as well as step-by-step direct instruction, so give minimal instruction and lots of encouragement.

Building a cardboard castle provides the opportunity to learn new words. After the castles are constructed, have the children identify the following castle-related words:

Battlement: A wall, notched for shooting, that screens soldiers from the enemy.

Drawbridge: A hinged bridge attached to the gatehouse that is raised and lowered over the moat.

Gatehouse: The tower containing the gate of the castle grounds.

Moat: A body of water surrounding the castle walls.

Pennant: A long, narrow flag that is emblazoned with the symbols for the castle occupant.

LANGUAGE ARTS ACTIVITY

▪ *Architect's Sketchbook*

Have your students or group members start a sketchbook and/or photo album of architectural details. Have them research, search for, sketch, or photograph:

Styles: Gothic, Baroque, Neoclassic, Classic, Colonial

Roof styles: mansard, gable gambrel, flat

Doorway styles and parts: lintel, ledged, braced, flush, paneled

Column styles: Tuscan, Doric, Gothic

Window styles: eyebrow, double hung, rose, picture, mansard, and fanlights

Molding: dentil, acanthus, chevron

Hardware: door hinges, doorknobs, thresholds

POEM

Sandburg, Carl. "Skyscraper." In *Imaginary Gardens* edited by Charles Sullivan. Harry N. Abrams, 1989.

Lee, Dennis. "Skyscraper." In *Read Aloud Poems for the Very Young* selected by Jack Prelutsky. Knopf, 1989.

VOCABULARY GROWTH WORDS

Apse: In church architecture, the rounded extension of the structure.

Architrave: In classical structures featuring columns, it is the horizontal beam resting on the columns.

Balustrade: A row of equally sized columns supporting a railing or architrave.

Buttress: A structure built against a wall to keep it from falling outward.

Column: A tall, vertical weight-supporting element of a building.

Crenellations: The squared notches at the top of castle towers and battlements.

Cupola: A circular construction at the top of a roof; it is often capped with a semispherical shape. Some cupolas were once used as lookouts while others contained a light. Cupolas also provide natural light to the interior of the building.

Lintel: The crosspiece at the top of the door.

Nave: The wide central aisle of a cathedral.

Piers: Heavy, load-bearing columns.

Pilasters: A supporting column that extends or juts out from a wall.

Pillar: A slender, vertical support.

Transept: In church architecture, the part that crosses the nave to form a cross.

Truss: The triangular-shaped supports of a roof.

Vault: An arched roof.

RESOURCES

J. B. Speed Art Museum
2035 South Third Street
Louisville, KY 40208
502-634-2700

    J. B. Speed Art Museum features an interactive exhibit titled "Architexture," where children can build structures and entire cities.

The American Architectural Foundation
1735 New York Avenue Northwest
Washington D.C. 20006
http://www.amerarchfoundation.com

    This nonprofit public outreach and educational organization maintains a Web site that includes a link titled "Learning by Design." It provides a series of K–12 curriculum supplements.

READ MORE ABOUT IT

Gibbons, Gail. *How a House Is Built.* Holiday House, 1990. Unpaged. (P)

    Gibbons lines up the entire house building team to give young readers a realistic notion of how many trades people it takes to build a wood frame house. Then, step by step, she takes the reader through the process: digging the hole for the foundation, placing the footings, bolting down the sill, putting up the sheathing, and installing heat ducts. As each step is illustrated, the building team members are shown doing their parts.

    After reading this book, adults may want to take children to the nearest building site several times, so they are able to see the real thing happening over time. A call to the local Habitat for Humanity or contractors' union may yield the necessary information.

Pratt, Paula Bryant. *Architecture*. Lucent Books, 1995. 112p. (I)

Essentially a history book, the text is divided by the major historical architecture time periods: the ancient world, the middle ages, Gothic, Renaissance, eighteenth and nineteenth centuries, modern, and contemporary architecture. At the same time, the author introduces the reader to important concepts and techniques such as tracery, incrustation, peristyle, and clerestory by incorporating them into her narrative. Pratt explains the social and historical forces on architecture. She intersperses her text with quotes and sidebars of outstanding historians, sociologists, and architects. Smoothly written and easy to follow, this book will appeal to curious young students of architecture.

Shemie, Bonnie. *Houses of China*. Tundra Books, 1996. 24p. Illustrated by Bonnie Shemie. (I)

Before the architectural variety of houses has been replaced by modern McDonald's sameness, Shemie wants her readers to learn about yurts, courtyard houses, stilt houses, and Hakka fort houses. The author describes the belief systems, such as Feng Shui, and natural forces that influence the design of these homes. For youth leaders seeking ways to enhance multicultural elements in their instruction, this is an excellent book.

Venturo, Piero. *Houses*. Houghton Mifflin, 1993. 64p. (P–I)

The history, styles, and variety of housing are described in Venturo's book. His illustrations, drawn from a variety of perspectives, give the reader overviews, side views, and cut-away views of houses. Once readers begin to look closely at the illustrations, they will catch on to the illustrator's humor. He shows people through the ages doing ordinary day-to-day activities within their homes. Venturo focuses on the interaction between materials and people's ways of living. There is an anthropological perspective to this book that is one of a series dealing with man's interaction with his environment. An excellent glossary is included.

Wood, Richard. *Architecture*. Thomson Learning, 1995. 48p. (I)

Basic architecture is described from a historical point of view. The author's purpose—exploring architectural legacies—is stated on the first pages. Wood points out that a legacy is something that is handed down to us from our predecessors. In this book, modern architecture is portrayed as a legacy from ancient worlds. Multicultural in scope, the book tells of the architectural legacies of ancient Egypt, Greece, ancient northern Europe, and Asia for example. The author compares and contrasts the building designs of ancient people with contemporary design. For example, he shows the similarities of Iraq's ancient ziggurats with the Chrysler building; the temples of Greece to the City Hall of Birmingham, England; and the timber framing and reed thatch roof of today's French cottages to Celtic building design. Throughout the text, the author draws comparisons between ancient and modern architectural design, thus fulfilling his intent to demonstrate the legacies from earlier civilizations.

2
BIRDS

Ornithology, the serious study of birds and their habits, progresses from the pastime of observing birds as they cavort, feed, and nest around apartment balconies, backyards and parks. As children begin to ask, "What bird is that?" they are starting to be interested in nature and their environment. From watching birds, boys and girls learn valuable facts about biology, zoology, and ecology. Knowledge of habitat, feeding habits, nesting behavior, territoriality, and species identification are some of the several scientific skills that boys and girls may acquire as they build their powers of observation while attracting and watching birds.

Elementary school teacher, biologist, nature center director, ornithologist, ecologist, birdseed entrepreneur, and children's book illustrator are a few of the jobs attractive to bird watchers. As with so many hobbies, bird-watching provides an opportunity to become involved with others and form friendships with those who share this interest. People have an instant circle of friends when, as adults they move to a new town and join the local Audubon club.

Ehlert, Lois. *Feathers for Lunch*. Harcourt Brace, 1990. Unpaged. Illustrated by Lois Ehlert. (P)

The cat is out and the birds are in jeopardy as he seeks a tasty lunch; however, his jingling bell saves the birds. At the book's end there is an identification chart to help readers identify the birds that gather at their bird feeder. Lois Ehlert's vibrant collages and illustrations of humorous cat expressions produce an enjoyable book experience.

8 ■ *2—BIRDS*

HOBBY STARTER ACTIVITY

■ *Bird Feeders*

Materials

Plastic 2-liter soda bottles
Birdseed
Mesh onion bags
Suet
Sunflower seeds
Millet
Dried berries
Cracked corn
Thistle seed
Wooden dowels ($\frac{1}{8}$")
Plastic wrap
Rubber bands

Using the materials listed above and the information provided in the chart below, have your group construct a variety of bird feeders. Have the children place them around your family home or group meeting area or neighborhood.

Birds	Type of Feeder	Feed
Nuthatches, flickers, thrushes, chickadees	Mesh onion bags (not the plastic kind with phony netting printed on them)	Suet and suet mixed with seed and dried berries
Quail, mourning doves, juncos	The ground	Millet, cracked corn, sunflower seeds
Nuthatches, finches, chickadees, redwing blackbirds, cardinals, blue jays	Recycled, 2-liter plastic soda bottles with tiny holes punched into the sides and dowels for perches stuck through the sides	Millet, cracked sunflower seeds, cracked peanuts, thistle seeds
Finches	Thistle seed feeders. Paper towel tubing with tiny holes punched all over. Push $\frac{1}{8}$" wooden dowels on pencils through the sides for perches. Cover the bottom with plastic wrap or aluminum foil secured with a rubber band	Thistle seeds
Hummingbirds	Nectar feeder bottle. A 1- or 2-liter soda bottle hung by cords at a slant so the nectar comes just to the lip but does not drip out	Nectar made from a mixture of sugar and water in a ratio of one part sugar to four parts of water. Mix and boil for a few minutes to make a light syrup

LANGUAGE ARTS ACTIVITY

▣ *Diamante*

Diamante is a highly structured type of poem. It follows a strict form that, when followed, results in a diamond shape, thus, its name.

First line: One noun or the topic of the poem
Second line: Two words describing the topic; adjectives
Third line: Three participles (*-ing* words) related to the topic
Fourth line: A four-word phrase
Fifth line: Three participles
Sixth line: Two adjectives
Seventh line: A synonym for the first noun

Example

Red-Bird
Brilliant, Scarlet
Cheering, Chirping, Chirruping
Joyful Peaked Cap Songster
Brightening, Entertaining, Singing
Rogue, Bright
Cardinal

Have your group members follow the diamante pattern to write bird-related or bird-watching poems. Once the poems are written, have them rewritten in their "best dress" and illustrated. Display on a bulletin board or in a group book.

POEM

Sandburg, Carl. "Look at Six Eggs." In *V Is for Verses* by Odille Ousley. Ginn, 1964.

VOCABULARY GROWTH WORDS

Audubon: John James Audubon was a famous illustrator of birds. Today the Audubon Society is an organization that studies and protects birds.

Camouflage: The pattern created by a bird's colors and feather design that blend the bird with its surroundings, making it difficult for predators to capture.

Colony: A large flock of birds living together.

Gizzard: A bird has no teeth to grind food into the pulpy mass needed for digestion. Instead a bird has a gizzard, a very muscular internal body part containing little stones and sand that the bird uses to grind food.

Mate: One of a pair of birds.

Ornithologist: A person who studies birds and their habits.

Plumage: A bird's feathers. The color and pattern of each variety of bird marks the bird as a member of that species.

Preening: The act of oiling and grooming feathers to keep them waterproof and in good condition. The bird uses the oil from the preen gland to do this.

Primaries: The strong outer feathers of a bird's wing. Being strong and flexible, they help to propel the bird in flight.

Range: The geographical boundaries of the territory in which the bird lives and migrates.

Secondaries: The feathers that are closest to the bird's body. These form a curved surface that gives the wing lift.

Look for additional vocabulary words in the glossaries of the books listed in the "Read More About It" section.

RESOURCES

National Audubon Society
700 Broadway
New York, NY 10003-9526
http://www.audubon.org

According to NAS, its mission is "to conserve and restore natural ecosystems, focusing on birds and other wildlife for the benefit of humanity and the earth's biological diversity." Teachers, parents, and group leaders are invited to use its environmental education program titled, "The Audubon Adventures Classroom Kit." The Audubon Web site includes a link titled "Kids & Education," a fun-filled site valuable to children as well as adults.

National Wildlife Federation
11100 Wildlife Center Drive
Reston, VA 20109
http://www.nwf.org/

According to NWF, its mission is "to educate, inspire, and assist individuals and organizations of diverse cultures to conserve wildlife and other natural resources and to protect the earth's environment in order to achieve a peaceful, equitable, and sustainable future." Provides a link to Ranger Rick's Kid Zone.

READ MORE ABOUT IT

Harrison, George. *Garden Birds of America*. Willow Creek Press, 1996. 160p. (I)

    Grown-ups and children will have a tug-of-war wanting to read this beautiful book. If you were not interested in bird-watching as a hobby, you would be after reading this book. Lively writing and gorgeous photographs enrich the topic and invite the reader to learn more. In addition to glamour shots of sixty popular backyard birds, the author provides photographs and descriptions of eleven gardens constructed specifically for bird attraction. Practical how-to information for building houses, feeders, birdbaths, and environments is included. At the back of the book, Harrison provides the directions and forms for registering gardens as wildlife habitats.

Jonas, Ann. *Bird Talk*. Greenwillow Books, 1999. 32p. (P)

    Anyone who has hung around avid bird-watchers knows that they have near folkloric ways to remember bird songs. For example, the towhee admonishes us to "Drink your tea." Ann Jonas has collected these mnemonic devices that bird-watchers are so fond of into a humorous book for the very young ornithologist.

Milord, Susan. *Bird Tales from Near to Far*. Williamson Publishing, 1999. 96p. Illustrated by Linda S. Wingerter. (P–I)

    Milord has collected bird-related tales from many countries and cultures. She combines the stories with delightful activities. Children are sure to enjoy making a quill pen, nesting boxes, and a decorated egg. The lists of materials are easy to locate; Milord has placed them in highlighted boxes. Storytellers will find added attractions to enrich storytelling programs.

Pine, Jonathan. *Backyard Birds*. HarperCollins, 1993. 48p. Illustrated by Julie Zickefoose. (P)

    This sweet book is illustrated in an old-fashioned style with watercolor and gouache from real-life subjects by Julie Zickefoose. Limited to six commonly seen birds, this book is the perfect size for a young bird-watcher. Pine's detailed yet easy-to-navigate text provides information about nesting, habits, feeding preferences, and identifying markings.

Ricciuti, Edward. *Birds*. Blackbird Press, 1993. 64p. (I)

    Written for the older child, this book uses photographs and diagrams to introduce the life and habits of birds to boys and girls. A scientific approach is used throughout the text that emphasizes biological information. The birds' life cycle, metabolism, and body part functions are detailed.

Spaulding, Dean T. *Feeding Our Feathered Friends.* Lerner Publications, 1997. 56p. (P–I)

      How to attract birds into your view with a great variety of food and feeders is the book's premise. Directions for making various feeders (e.g., from egg cartons, milk cartons, or tennis balls) are provided. Of them all, the stiff shirt feeder is the cleverest. Readers are advised to make $\frac{1}{8}$" slits in shirtsleeves, stuff them with birdseed, tie the shirt, and hang the shirt on a tree limb. Photographs and diagrams make the information more accessible to the young reader.

3
CATS

Nothing teaches a child the meaning of love, care, compassion, and companionship as living with and caring properly for a pet. It is one of life's great mysteries why cats choose to live and be loyal to humans, but they do, and humans are the better for it.

Children learn the satisfaction of watering, feeding, grooming, cleaning up after, and playing with this highly interactive animal that shows its appreciation in purrs and snuggles. Caring for cats leads to careers in veterinary medicine, animal control work, therapy, pet store business, zoo animal caretaker, and show business.

Barber, Antonia. *The Mousehole Cat*. Aladdin Paperbacks, 1996. Unpaged. Illustrated by Nicola Bayley. (P–I)

This is a charming story to read aloud at Christmastime. It is the story of Mowzer, a cat, who has a fisherman, Tom. Mowzer has several children whom she does not visit often because she does not think they have trained their people well. Life is good for Mowzer. Tom feeds her morgy-broth, kedgeree, grilled fairmaids, and star-gazy pie. All is well until one winter there comes a terrible storm; the fishing fleet cannot leave the harbor to fish. The families of Mousehole are hungry and Christmas is coming. Tom decides that he needs to make the attempt to venture forth to bring back a catch of fish. Mowzer is determined to accompany him, and it's a good thing. The sweetness of her singing calms the Great Storm Cat. Tom and Mowzer sail back into the harbor with a large catch of fish and a great feast takes place.

HOBBY STARTER ACTIVITY

▪ *Adopt a Kitty, Share a Cat*

Take your students to an animal shelter to pick out a kitty to adopt. An alternative is to provide foster care for a cat or kitten until it can be adopted. The Humane Society in many communities needs volunteers to support this service. When you and the children have socialized the cat with lots of play and loving, you may wish to take the children and the cat on regular visits to your local nursing home in order to provide the joy of a reprieve from loneliness that a well-socialized cat and children can give.

LANGUAGE ARTS ACTIVITY

▪ *Feline Photos*

Cats and kittens make wonderful photo subjects, but they are not obedient, docile models. They have to be caught on camera by a patient photographer. You would not want to invest in expensive cameras and film for this project, but inexpensive alternatives, such as instant cameras on sale, may do.

Have your students photograph their cats. Display the photographs on a bulletin board or in an album. Encourage the children to make up whimsical quotations to accompany the cats' expressions.

POEM

Larrick, Nancy. *Cats Are Cats*. Philomel, 1988. Drawings by Ed Young.
    Select any poem to read aloud to the group.

Keillor, Garrison. *Cat, You Better Come Home*. Puffin, 1995. Illustrated by Steve Johnson and Lou Fancher.

VOCABULARY GROWTH WORDS

Carnivorous: Meat-eating animals such as cats.

Catnip: A mint plant that attracts cats.

Distemper: A deadly disease that strikes cats and is characterized by fever.

Hair balls: Hair clumps in the stomach that the cat will cough up usually when visitors come calling.

Litter: The baby kittens born of one mother.

Purebred: A cat of a recognized breed.

Rabies: A potentially deadly infectious disease that may cause choking.

Territory: A cat's chosen area.

Vaccinations: Shots that the vet gives to cats to prevent diseases.

Vibrissae: Whiskers that are sensitive to touch.

RESOURCES

American Cat Fanciers Association
P.O. Box 203
Point Lookout, MO 65726
www.acfacat.com
   The American Cat Fanciers Association's primary functions are the administration of cat shows and the education of the general public about domesticated cats.

READ MORE ABOUT IT

Cole, Joanna. *My New Kitten*. Morrow Junior Books, 1996. Unpaged. Photographs by Margaret Miller. (P)
   Margaret Miller's color photographs provide the substance of this book. Cole's text recounts the birth and development of a litter of kittens from a little girl's point of view. The photo-essay focuses primarily on how the mother cat takes care of her litter until at the end of the eight weeks, the little girl takes her kitten of choice home with her.

Gutman, Bill. *Becoming Your Cat's Best Friend*. Millbrook Press, 1997. 64p. Drawings by Anne Canevari Green. (P–I)
   Anne Canevari Green's cartoons embellish Gutman's text, which provides the history, characteristics, and care of cats. Gutman makes a point to compare and contrast pet behavior to wild animal behavior. For example, because a cat in the wild does not submit to a leader, it is counterproductive to discipline it, as you might a dog. An angry owner results in the cat leaving home or sulking. Building the cat's trust is critical to a happy cat. Gutman tells the reader how to become a cat's best friend.

Higgins, Maria Mihalik. *Cats: From Tigers to Tabbies*. Discovery Channel, 1998. 64p. (P–I)
   Clever language use, wildlife action shots, and cute kitty photos compose this book that compares wild felines with domesticated cats. Feeding and hunting habits, behavior, tails, fur, and the seeing and smelling habits of tigers and domesticated cats are compared. Historical fun facts are scattered throughout.

Ivory, Lesley Anne. *Meet My Cats*. Dial, 1989. Unpaged. (P–I)

This celebrated illustrator shares her elegant portraits of her cats with us in this richly illustrated book. Cats and kittens are portrayed in paintings that range from glamour shots to comic poses. Precious little vignettes about each cat's adventures within the artist's family accompany their charming portraits. For the cat and art lover this is a beautiful album-like picture book.

Kelsey-Wood, Dennis, and Eve Kelsey-Wood. *Choosing the Perfect Cat*. Chelsea House, 1997. 65p. (I)

In glossy photographs and detailed text, the authors describe the many cat breeds. The cats described include the Manx, the Burmese, the Scottish, and the Japanese Bobtail among many others. This book is intended for readers who want to purchase or learn more about a specific breed. Cautions are given about making sure that everyone in the household really wants the responsibility of cat ownership.

4 DANCING

On their way to having fun by participating in tap dance, ballet, line, ballroom, folk, swing, and jazz dance, boys and girls may pick up expertise in rhythm, social skills, music, popular culture, gracefulness, co-ordination, and self expression. Because all the world's peoples love to dance, a study of dance leads children to discover the moves of other cultures and to join in the dance.

Dance therapist, dance studio owner, actor, talent agent, professional dancer, dance instructor, show business impresario, dance historian, and choreographer are just some of the careers that result from an earlier interest in dancing.

Gray, Libba Moore. *My Mama Had a Dancing Heart*. Orchard Books, 1995. Unpaged. Illustrated by Raul Colon. (P)

In beautiful, lyrical style, Gray recounts the remembrances of a little girl whose mother loved to dance. The little girl tells how her mother loved to greet each season of the year by inviting her little girl to join her in a celebration of twirling, knee-slapping, galloping delights of movement. After each exuberant dance, there was a quiet mother/daughter time of sharing a beverage, thus the text itself has its own rhythm. Raul Colon's etchings and watercolor washes executed in a warm, muted palette reflect the warmth of the subject.

HOBBY STARTER ACTIVITY

▪ *It's 5/25! Time to Jig and Jive!*

It's National Tap Dance Day, so celebrate! Invite a local dance instructor to teach your group a simple tap dancing step to celebrate National Tap Dance Day on May 25. An alternative would be to rent or borrow a videotape, have the children tape pennies to the their sneaker bottoms and dance. On a regular basis, get your group together to learn new steps and have fun.

LANGUAGE ARTS ACTIVITY

▪ *A Dancing Poetry Bulletin Board*

Poetry and dancing are natural mates. Both express human emotions with rhythm, cadence, and meter. Have your children search the Internet, library shelves, and the *Index to Poetry for Children and Young People* for dance-related poems. Have the children copy the poems onto curvy, wavy banner shapes. Display the group's dance-related poems on a bulletin board with rolling hills pictured in the background. Have the children draw dancing stick figures onto the background. Attach the poetry banners to look as though the stick figures are holding the poems and dancing across the hills!

POEM

Jabar, Cynthia. *Shimmy Shake Earthquake: Don't Forget to Dance.* Little Brown, 1992.
Select any poem to read aloud to your group.

VOCABULARY GROWTH WORDS

Accent: The emphasis given to a particular beat in a musical measure.

Ball-change: A basic dance movement that calls for two weight changes. First, step back on the ball of the foot then step forward to put the weight on the ball of the other foot.

Ballroom dance: A dance done with a partner. The waltz, polka, samba, tango, and foxtrot are examples of ballroom dances.

Choreography: The serious study of dance. The plan of a dance such as a ballet.

Downbeat: The first count in a musical measure.

Free foot: In dance, the foot with no weight on it.

Jig: A lively dance performed with springy steps.

Supporting foot: In dance, the foot bearing the dancer's weight.

Tempo: How fast or slow the music's played.

Upbeat: The "and" count when dancers begin to move, it is actually the last count of a musical measure.

RESOURCES

National Dance Association
1900 Association Drive
Reston, VA 20191
http://www.aahperd.org/nda
  According to the National Dance Association, its purpose is "to increase knowledge, improve skills, and encourage sound professional practices in dance education through high-quality dance programs."

READ MORE ABOUT IT

Ancona, George. *Let's Dance!* Morrow Junior Books, 1998. Unpaged. (P)
  Ancona's peppy photographs capture the joy of dancing; his text explains the concepts. The universal love and value of dance among the world's many cultures are described. This happy book reflects Ancona's love for dancing and his desire to pass it along to the younger generation. He insists to his readers that if they can kick, step, leap, and wiggle, they can dance.

Grau, Andree. *Dance.* Eyewitness Books. Alfred A. Knopf, 1998. 60p. (P–I)
  With an emphasis on cross-cultural themes, Grau introduces young dancers to the worlds of dance. At the same time Grau defines the concepts and terminology associated with dance, for example, the use of masks, the expressions of strength and beauty, the costumes, and the telling of tales. The relationship between dance and religion is explained. Dance from many perspectives can be found here.

Hamanaka, Sheila. *The Hokey Pokey.* Simon & Schuster, 1997. 32p. Illustrated by Sheila Hamanaka. (P)
  Sometime during the 1950s, three musicians, Larry La Prise, Charles P. Macak, and Taftt Baker wrote "The Hokey Pokey," a song and dance meant for posterity. Sheila Hamanaka's energetic, colorful illustrations bring this fifties dance tune into the twenty-first century. This is an arm-shaking, leg-twisting song and dance book that will get your children movin' and groovin'.

Hart, Avery, and Paul Mantell. *Kids Make Music!: Clapping & Tapping from Bach to Rock!* Williamson Publishing, 1993. Illustrated by Loretta Trezzo Braren. 156p. (P–I)

    Let's do the Dinosaur Dance! Glue pennies on your sneakers, count in fours and learn to do the Time Step. Want to do something smooth? Try the Moon Walk. Go Hispanic and dance the flamenco. All these dances plus ballet, hip-hop and Native American dances are described. Easy-to-follow dance directions are given from page 46 to 57. Get up and dance, dance, dance.

Tythacott, Louise. *Dance.* Thomson Learning, 1995. 48p. (I)

    Photographs capture the facial expressions and movements of dancers from many countries and cultures. History and trends in dance are described. The various cultural reasons for a dance are given, such as helping a pregnant woman give birth, blessing a place, bringing good luck, and communicating with the spirit world. For those leaders looking for ways to focus on dance's diverse appeal, this is the book.

5
DOGS

Chumming around with a dog teaches boys and girls what it means to nurture, groom, play with, and teach an animal. Patience and compassion blend together to bond dog and child.

These new skills can later be extended to training working dogs such as dogs for the blind and deaf, herding dogs, sled dogs, rescue dogs, and police dogs.

Careers growing out of dog care are dog trainer, rescue work, police work, veterinary medicine, therapy, show business, breeder, animal control work, and dog show production.

Rathmann, Peggy. *Officer Buckle and Gloria*. G. P. Putnam's Sons, 1995. Unpaged. Illustrated by Peggy Rathmann. (P)

Officer Buckle bombs as a spokesperson for safety until Gloria, the department's new police dog accompanies him. Unbeknownst to Officer Buckle, Gloria stands behind him and demonstrates the safety tips given by Officer Buckle. Gloria's tricks delight the children and Officer Buckle comes to believe that they loved his safety tips speech until he sees a video of one of the performances. When he realizes that Gloria has captivated the audience, he becomes so disheartened that he can no longer work. Gloria performs on stage by herself and guess what? She bombs! The audience goes to sleep. Officer Buckle and Gloria discover that teamwork pays off. Together they succeed.

HOBBY STARTER ACTIVITY

▪ *Celebrate Working Dogs—National Dog Week September 19–25*

Gloria is a working dog. Have the children in your group find out about the working dogs in your neighborhood. Have them make inquiries by contacting 4-H Clubs that train working dogs; cattle and sheep ranchers who have dogs; senior citizen centers that have companion dogs; the police department; the Society for the Blind; or your county Social Services Agency that knows blind, deaf, physically handicapped, and epileptic people who own dogs that assist them. Invite these people and their dogs to your group for a celebration of working dogs. Have your students interview the people beforehand so that each is prepared to give an introductory vignette about the dog and its owner on the day of the celebration. Appoint one child to be the emcee to move the program along. Serve dog biscuits to the dogs and punch and cookies to the humans. Here's a dog biscuit recipe:

Fidough Biscuits

Ingredients

2 cups whole wheat flour
¼ cup soy flour
¼ cup cornmeal
½ cup powdered milk
1 tablespoon dried parsley flakes (for doggy breath)
6 Tablespoons shortening
1 egg beaten
½ cup ice water (add more water if needed to make a stiff dough)

Directions

1. Preheat the oven to 350 degrees.
2. Grease a cookie sheet.
3. Combine flours, cornmeal, powdered milk, and dried parsley flakes.
4. Cut in the shortening.
5. Add the beaten egg.
6. Add the ice water a bit at a time until the mixture forms a ball.
7. Roll out to ½-inch thickness.
8. Cut with dog biscuit cutter.
9. Place on the cookie sheet.
10. Bake for 30 minutes.

LANGUAGE ARTS ACTIVITY

▪ *Dog Name Chart*

People love to give their dogs interesting (most of the time) names. Have your group members interview neighborhood dog owners to discover the reasons behind the dogs' names. Duplicate this chart and distribute it.

Dog's Name	Dog's Breed	Dog's Characteristics	Reason Owner Gave for Name	Your Opinion (Is it appropriate? Why or why not?)

POEM

>Livingston, Myra Cohn. *Dog Poems*. Holiday House, 1990.
>Select any poem to read aloud to your group.

VOCABULARY GROWTH WORDS

>**Breed:** A group of dogs descended from a common ancestor.
>
>**Canine:** That family of carnivores consisting of wolves, foxes, jackals, and dogs.
>
>**Crossbreed:** A dog descended from a mix of ancestors; a mongrel.
>
>**Housebroken:** A dog trained to live in a house.
>
>**Litter:** The group of puppies born by a dog.
>
>**Mongrel:** A dog of several breeds.
>
>**Muzzle:** The projecting part of a dog's head containing nose, mouth, and snout.
>
>**Obedience training:** The process of teaching a dog to follow commands.
>
>**Purebred:** A dog that belongs to a breed the characters of which have been maintained over generations.
>
>**Socialization:** The process of introducing a dog to unfamiliar people, places, and pets in order for it to learn appropriate behavior for living among human groups.

RESOURCES

American Kennel Club
5580 Centerview Drive
Raleigh, NC 27606
http://www.akc.org
   This Web site provides a complete listing of AKC-sponsored events; educational information about dog ownership (e.g., selection, healthcare), purebred dogs and registration; feature articles; board meeting reports; and dog-related legislation. A Kids' Corner page is also included.

Guide Dogs for the Blind
P.O. Box 151200
San Rafael, CA 94915-1200
1-800 295-4050
http://www.guidedogs.com
   This site provides a wealth of information including volunteer opportunities, puppy raising, and tips on how to become a professional trainer.

READ MORE ABOUT IT

Gibbons, Gail. *Dogs*. Holiday House, 1996. 32p. Illustrated by Gail Gibbons. (P)
   Gibbons illustrates and writes in simple text her recounting of the history, types of breeds, habits, and characteristics of dogs. A section explaining how to care for your dog included. The last page showcases famous dogs from Sater, the heroic watchdog of ancient Greece, to Beethoven, the movie star.

McMains, Joel M. *Dog Training Projects for Young People*. Howell Book House, 1995. 280p. (I)
   For the older child this book is a fact-filled compendium of obedience training techniques. McMains takes the novice dog trainer through an instructional sequence. The goal of the book is to help the dog owner have a dog so well trained that it could be entered in a dog show.

Otto, Carolyn. *Our Puppies Are Growing*. HarperCollins, 1998. 32p. Illustrated by Mary Morgan. (P)
   Part of the Let's Read and Find Out Science series, this easy-to-read book decorated with soft, warm illustrations by Mary Morgan, recounts the birth and growth of puppies as seen through the eyes of a little girl. Eleven extension activities are listed on the last page. Children will find out a lot more about dogs by doing these activities with adult encouragement.

Paulsen, Gary. *My Life in Dog Years*. Delacorte Press, 1998. 137p. (I)
   Popular children's author Gary Paulsen supplies us with vignettes about the dog friends that have been so big a part of his life. We learn of Cookie who saved his life and Quincy who brought zaniness to his life. Readers are at once wiping away tears and stifling guffaws as they read this heartwarming collection of stories about a man and his dogs.

Ring, Elizabeth. *Companion Dogs: More Than Best Friends*. Millbrook Press, 1994. 32p. (P–I)
   In this photographic essay that is part of a series, Good Dogs, Ring tells how dogs are trained for therapy and companionship. The text is salted with anecdotes and success stories about dogs changing individual lives for the better.

Rosen, Michael J. *Kid's Best Dog Book*. Workman, 1993. 128p. (I)
   Michael Rosen has written a compilation of fascinating facts about dog nature and how this nature affects the timing and manner of training. A comprehensive book, it covers care, feeding, growth, and development, as well as techniques of training. Tone of voice, pace of training, consistency, and understanding are stressed. If Rosen's guidelines are followed, a happy, well-trained family dog is sure to result.

6
DRAWING AND PAINTING

Drawing and painting, like all the hobbies in this book, have the possibility to bring a lifetime of joy and satisfaction as well as a profession. As boys and girls experiment with various media and art projects, they hone their knowledge of the elements and principles of design. Playing with color, pattern, line, shape, and design develops their artistic skills and eyes, as well as their creativity.

Careers such as graphic layout artist, interior decorator, fashion designer, theatrical set designer, fine artist, graphic artist, book illustrator, cartoonist, and art therapist are open to the young artist.

dePaola, Tomie. *The Art Lesson*. G. P. Putnam's Sons, 1989. 32p. Illustrated by Tomie dePaola. (P)

Tommy loves to draw. He draws pictures everywhere: on paper, on walls, even on the bed sheets. His cousins are studying to be artists. They tell him never to copy. His mom and dad proudly paste his drawings around the house and at dad's business. When he becomes a first-grader, he looks forward to the arrival of Mrs. Bowers, the art teacher, and his first real art lesson. Tommy learns that art lessons squelch self-expression and demand copying. Tommy stands up for the rights of self-expression and wins a compromise from his teachers. The book is illustrated in dePaola's unerring simple style.

HOBBY STARTER ACTIVITY

▪ *The More They Draw, the Better They Draw*

Prize-winning illustrator Janet Stevens suggested in a speech that one of the best ways to increase children's confidence when drawing and painting is to supply them with plenty of free, inexpensive paper. In this manner, the children are free to persevere despite dissatisfaction with what they produce. Children can simply ball up their rejects, throw them out, and start anew. When hovering adults aren't nervous about reams of precious, expensive art paper being wasted, the young artists can practice until they are satisfied with their artwork.

Sources of free paper may be found in offices, print shops, newspaper offices, and anywhere computers are used. So commandeer your friends to be on the lookout for recycle bins and boxes filled with reusable paper. Encourage your young artists to draw and color to their satisfaction. Art supplies are available from Daniel Smith Art Supply, 1-800-426-7925.

LANGUAGE ARTS ACTIVITY

▪ *Art Talks*

Once the children in your group have a small collection of paintings and drawings with which they are satisfied, have them share their paintings with each other. Have them talk about the paintings and drawings. When people talk about their art they describe it in terms of the effect desired and the colors that were used—bright, muted, jewel tone, or pastel. They describe the forms used—rounded, asymmetrical, branched, triangular, or nature-based. They describe the subject—portrait, abstract, or still life. They describe the lines used—jagged, horizontal, or vertical. Artists talk about the pattern in their paintings—wavy, striped, dotted, floral, or lined. They speak of the feelings that they wanted to convey. Encourage your students to describe their paintings using terms of color, line, form, subject, pattern, and feeling.

POEM

Elledge, Scott. "The Paint Box." In *Wider Than the Sky: Poems to Grow Up With*. Harper & Row, 1990.

VOCABULARY GROWTH WORDS

Abstract expressionism: A type of art that is nonrepresentational in composition.

Caricature: A humorous, distorted likeness of an object, person, or animal.

Easel: An artist's device for holding the artist's canvas or picture on display.

Elements of design: Form, space, texture, line, and color.

Engrave: To cut a design into a surface.

Impressionism: A type of art in which the artist paints in short strokes to show changes of light.

Landscape: A picture that depicts natural scenery such as a prairie or meadow.

Palette: A board on which an artist arranges or mixes colors; the color choices for a picture that an artist makes.

Palette knife: A flexible metal blade that the artist uses to mix and/or apply paint.

Perspective: Pictures drawn to show the effect of distance and depth on the represented objects.

Tempera: Pigments that are mixed with sizing to produce a dull finish; also commonly known as poster paint.

RESOURCES

Crayola.com
http://www.crayola.com

Binney & Smith maintains this Web site, which provides children, parents, and teachers with a wealth of arts and crafts activity ideas using Crayola products. Lesson plans are provided for teachers. Children are invited to publish their artwork, poems, and stories.

READ MORE ABOUT IT

Heller, Ruth. *Color*. Grosset & Dunlap, 1995. Unpaged. (P–I)

Fun with color appears on each page under the magic of Heller's creative playing with both words and colors. The use of colored acetate aids the reader in discovering what happens when color is blended, combined, or mixed. When young artists complete this book, they will know how color works.

Milord, Susan. *Adventures in Art*. Williamson Publishing, 1997. 160p. (I)

Children will glom onto this book like burdock on a wool sock. Written for the older child, it contains more than 100 art-related activities. Many media are represented, such as oil, watercolor, charcoal, and pastels, for starters. Many types of activities are described, such as collage, sculpture, mosaics, yarn, and cut paper. With materials and this book in hand, there will be no excuses for watching television.

Roche, Denis M. *Loo-Loo, Boo and Art You Can Do*. Houghton Mifflin, 1996. 32p. (P)

Bright, cartoon-like illustrations depict a variety of projects such as potato prints, sculpting, stinky clay, facemasks, crayon magic collage, and papier-mâché. Loo-Loo and Boo are characters from the Art 'Til Ya Drop television series. Excellent cleanup tips are given.

Sirett, Dawn. *My First Paint Book*. Dorling Kindersley, 1994. 47p. (P–I)

Easy-to-follow, step-by-step directions coupled with full-color photographs make this an ideal book for fun around the kitchen table. Beautiful, satisfying products are sure to result from reading this book. Some of these are marbled folders, stenciled T-shirts, papier-mâché pins, and painted bottles. Most materials are easily available around the house, but a trip to an art supply shop may be necessary to purchase the painting roller, brushes, papers, and fabric, poster, acrylic, and water-based paints required for successful completion of the projects. A great holiday or birthday gift for a child would be a box packed with this book and the supplies needed to craft the projects.

Yates, Irene. *All About Pattern*. Benchmark Books, 1998. 32p. (P)

The young artist's guide to perceiving pattern, this book will help any novice of art to see striped, checked, spotted, and wavy patterns all around. Patterns may be seen in plants, animals, and buildings. Readers are encouraged to take an observation walk to look for and draw patterns as they walk down a street. Directions for simple art projects that use patterns are given.

Yenawine, Philip. *Key Art Terms for Beginners*. New York: Harry N. Abrams, 1995. 160p. (I)

An alphabetical, as opposed to stylistic or historical, journey through the world of art, this book focuses on the terms and concepts associated with art. A wonderful reference, this book, diligently read, is sure to enlarge the reader's vocabulary. The young art student will be well beyond using the term "thingamajig" to describe art terms after using this book. Photographs of significant works of art generously illustrate the concepts and terms.

7
EGG DECORATION

Fine motor skills, knowledge of folklore and folk art, appreciation of pattern, and insight into symbolism result from an interest in egg decoration. Because of its cross-cultural and historical aspects, boys and girls may come to appreciate that this kitchen-table Easter activity has an unsuspected breadth and depth. Careers in decorative art, folk art, museum curator, and arts therapy are possibilities for children who take more than a passing interest in egg decoration.

Milhous, Katherine. *The Egg Tree*. Charles Scribner's Sons, 1950; Aladdin Paperbacks, 1992. Unpaged. Illustrated by Katherine Milhous. (P–I)

Caldecott Medal winner, *The Egg Tree* is a gently told story softly illustrated in muted colors. It is a recounting of two Easter mornings in Pennsylvania Dutch country. During the first morning, fancily painted eggs are discovered by Katy. This event leads to an egg-painting lesson from Grandmom. Soon the decorated eggs are displayed on a birch tree. The next year the tree is bigger and the egg decorations are more spectacular. People come from far and near to see the egg tree. Directions for making an egg tree are provided on the back cover.

HOBBY STARTER ACTIVITY

▪ *Create an Egg Tree*

Materials

Sand or small stones sufficient to fill a 2-pound coffee can
Large (2-pound) coffee can
Sturdy tree branch
Decorated hollow eggs
Ribbon

Directions

1. Pour sand or small stones into the coffee can until it is about half filled.
2. Anchor the tree branch in the sand or stones. Use the remaining sand or stones to fill the coffee can.
3. Make a loop of ribbon and knot the ends together.
4. Gingerly poke the loop through the hole at the fatter bottom end of the decorated hollow egg and push it through the hole at the top of the egg.
5. Decorate the tree branch with the eggs.

LANGUAGE ARTS ACTIVITY

▪ *Egg Tree Show and Tell*

Eggs are decorated with ancient symbols that have meaning. Some symbols were created circa 4000 B.C. Have your students research egg decorating books and encyclopedias to discover the various symbols and the significance of each. Using a wax resist technique, have them decorate blown-out eggs with the symbols. Have them explain the ethnic region of the symbols and their meanings whenever they show off the egg tree to each other, family, and/or community members.

An egg decorating kit that contains directions, beeswax, and a kistka (Luba's Ukrainian Egg Decorating Kit) may be ordered from Ukrainian Gift Shop, 2512 39th Ave. NE St. Anthony, MN 55421 or call (612) 788-2545.

POEM

Livingston, Myra Cohn. "Easter: For Penny." In *Michael Hague's Family Easter Treasury* edited by Michael Hague. Henry Holt, 1999. Illustrated by Michael Hague.

VOCABULARY GROWTH WORDS

Decorate: To paint designs on an object.

Kistka: A basic tool for Ukrainian decoration; it consists of a tiny pen-like funnel attached to a handle. Melted beeswax is applied to the egg with it. *Kistka* is the Ukrainian word for *little bone*.

Krashanky: These are hard-boiled eggs dyed one color, typically red.

Pagan: An ancient belief system that is based on nature. Many egg decorating symbols originated from pagan customs believed to originate around 4,000 B.C.

Pysanky: The Ukrainian name for raw multicolored decorated eggs. A Ukrainian myth holds that bad and evil occurrences will take place if pysanky are not created.

Red beets: They are not just for eating. Their juice makes a red dye for eggs traditional among Greeks.

Symbol: A graphic representation of a concept, belief, or country.

Ukrainian: Pertaining to the people and customs of the Ukraine, a country in Eastern Europe.

Wax resist: A decoration technique in which a design is drawn on the egg with melted wax; the egg is then dipped into a dye bath.

RESOURCES

Pysanka by Adriana
http://www.pysanka.com
   This Web site provides ideas and suggestions for decorating eggs in the traditional Ukrainian manner. Examples are shown. Decorated eggs and decorating supplies may be ordered from this site.

READ MORE ABOUT IT

Griffin, Margaret and Deborah Seed. *The Amazing Egg Book*. Addison-Wesley, 1989. 64p. (P–I)
   Margaret Griffin and Deborah Seed give away all the secrets about eggs including fish eggs. They discuss the myths associated with eggs as well as scientific facts. Customs associated with eggs are described. Play with words, recipes, and games lighten up the text to make this a highly entertaining, informative text.

Luciow, Johanna, Ann Kmit, and Loretta Luciow. *Eggs Beautiful: How to Make Ukrainian Easter Eggs*. Ukrainian Gift Shop, 1975. 96p. (I)

    Without this book in your collection, you are in danger of not knowing the history and magic attributed to the decorative egg. Without the tradition of decorating eggs, humankind is placed in jeopardy of being conquered and destroyed by evil according to ancient Hutzul (mountain people of Ukraine) tradition. In addition to the history and traditional folklore of Ukrainian egg decoration, symbolism of the designs is explained. The technicalities of decorating eggs are explained. Photographs of beautiful eggs show the possibilities for keeping this tradition alive.

Pollak, Jane. *Decorating Eggs*. Sterling Lark, 1996. 122p. (I–A)

    Written for the proficient egg decorator, this book is filled with advanced techniques. Featured is the kistka, a metal instrument shaped like a miniature funnel with a handle. This is the secret weapon with which the intricate design of Ukrainian egg decoration is accomplished. Beautiful photographs show off the symbolically decorated eggs.

Sechrist, Elizabeth Hough. "In the Easter Basket." In *Michael Hague's Family Easter Treasury* edited by Michael Hague. Henry Holt, 1999. pp. 81–88. Illustrated by Michael Hague. (I)

    Michael Hague's gorgeous illustrations capture the glorious joy and sweetness of Easter. He has collected old and new stories, essays, and poems to celebrate this holiday's pre-Christian and Christian origins. Included are classic pieces by Elizabeth Coatsworth, Oscar Wilde, and Alice Sligh Turnbull. Sechrist's essay tells of the historical and multicultural aspects of decorated eggs and uses of them, such as hunting, exchanging, tree decoration, and rolling.

Stalcup, Ann. *Ukrainian Egg Decoration: A Holiday Tradition*. PowerKids Press, 1999. 24p. (P–I)

    Egg decorating may be an ancient custom but here is an up-to-date book. Straightforward text and close-up photos make a complicated art form easy to understand. Combined with older books on the topic, it will help young enthusiasts increase their skills as they master creating symbolic designs with wax resist techniques. Directions for creating a very simple decorated egg are given. An excellent glossary is included. This book, one of a series titled Crafts of the World, is a welcome contribution to the literature of children's hobbies.

8
FACE PAINTING

At nearly every fair, fundraiser, community event, festival, and celebration there will be a lineup of children waiting for the touch of a face painter's brush. A popular hobby, face painting calls for fine motor coordination, artistic skill, and a responsible attitude. Patience combined with a sense of fun helps.

Because of its historical and multicultural qualities, face painting may arouse curiosity as to its uses across cultures and occupations. Children who become interested in face painting could extend that interest to cosmetologist, artist, theatrical work, Chinese opera artist, cross-cultural researcher, sociologist, anthropologist, clown, and professional event performer.

Falwell, Cathryn. *Clowning Around*. Orchard Books, 1991. Unpaged. Illustrated by Cathryn Falwell. (P)

Written for the preschool set, *Clowning Around* plays with words. The little clown rearranges letters to create different words on each page. Each page consists of two levels. The top level depicts the transmutation of the objects conjured up by the little clown as he manipulates the letters to create words on the lower level. A clown's makeup is a version of face painting thus the connection to this next hobby, face painting.

HOBBY STARTER ACTIVITY

▪ *Face Painting*

Materials

- Water-based safe facial paints and makeup
- Makeup spangles
- Towels
- Cold cream
- Facial tissues
- Cotton balls and swabs
- Soap and water

Have the children practice face painting on each other. Be obsessively certain that all materials are safe for facial skin. Establish hard and fast rules about the avoidance of using face paint around eyes.

When the children are ready, have them paint the faces of extremely willing younger children for whom you have obtained written parental permission to participate in this activity. For a reluctant child, have the face painters paint a symbol on the hand or ankle.

LANGUAGE ARTS ACTIVITY

▪ *Two-Column Dialogue*

Have the children pair up. Have each child paint the face of the other. Take a close-up Polaroid photograph of each child. Later, glue each photo to the top of a 12-by-18-inch paper folded in half lengthwise (one piece of paper per pair; one photo per column). Have the children imagine what the characters might say or write to each other and have them take turns writing back and forth on the two columns. This is not the time to fuss about perfect spelling; the children are just having fun with this activity.

POEM

Prelutsky, Jack. "Bring on the Clowns." In *Circus*. Aladdin Books, 1989. Pictures by Arnold Lobel.

VOCABULARY GROWTH WORDS

Base: Not a sports term. In face painting, base refers to the first color applied overall to the face. Decorative details are added to it.

Blend: A face painting technique in which a second color is applied to a first with a damp sponge, taking care to blur the line between the colors.

Cleansing: A very important part of face painting. First, all brushes, sponges, and water must be cleaned before you start. Be certain that the models clean their faces completely when the event is finished.

Cream makeup: Avoid these products. They are oil-based which makes them difficult to apply because it smudges easily and is difficult to remove.

Face painting: The craft of decorating faces to create disguises or for decoration.

Lien P'U: In Chinese opera makeup styles, it means, "the face that shows a record." This is taken to mean that the design of the makeup reveals the character.

Precaution: Safety measures taken before face painting is done. An important precaution is not to use red near eyes, for example.

Symmetrical: Exactly balanced design.

Water-based makeup: Makeup that is ideal for face painting. It dries quickly; it is easily used for fine lines and details. Best of all it cleans up easily.

Whiteface: A type of makeup in which white is used all over as the base. It is used for clowns, spacemen, spooks, and skulls.

RESOURCES

International Clown Hall of Fame
Grand Avenue Mall
161 West Wisconsin Ave., Suite LL700
Milwaukee, WI 53203
http://www.clownmuseum.org/

Located in Milwaukee, Wisconsin, this museum promotes laughter and honors outstanding clowns. Its Web site includes a history of clowns, a brief discussion of clown types, links to other clown-related Web sites, newsletters, and a virtual tour of the Hall of Fame.

READ MORE ABOUT IT

Editors of Klutz Press. *Face Painting*. Klutz Press, 1990. 65p. (I)

Face painting is not to be entered into without care and caution for eye and skin problems. The writers of this book give readers fair warning. Test for skin allergies and discontinue if a problem arises. Keep red paint away from eyes. There is no red pigment approved by the FDA for use near the eyes. Use water-based, nontoxic cosmetic paints. The authors recommend Kryolan GM6H because of its respected reputation in theatrical makeup. Having said that, the book details how to paint full characters in addition to symbols for hand, cheek, knees and feet painting. A chapter is devoted to Halloween faces such as Frankenstein. Various clown faces and costumes demonstrate the versatility of this art form, the purpose of which is to encourage silliness and fun.

Lincoln, Margaret. *Face Painting*. Copper Beech Books, 1997. 32p. (P–I)
   The author begins her book with a section on getting prepared with the proper assemblage of tools and materials. Techniques such as sponging and color mixing follow. How-to instructions explain and illustrate various characters such as super heroes, animals, aliens, and witches. A glossary is included.

Russon, Jacqueline. *Face Painting*. Thomson Learning, 1994. 32p. (P–I)
   Makeup artist Jacqueline Russon describes how to create 28 fantastic face designs. Especially wonderful are her Birds of a Feather, but others might find her The Seasons faces intriguing. Her ideas are unusual and the results attractive. Children wanting to put on a circus will find clown faces. Those who want to put on a play will find character faces such as an owl, a snow queen, and a busy bee. An added feature is her section on the history of makeup.

Russon, Jacqueline. *Face Painting*. Carolrhoda Books, 1997. 24p. (P)
   Ten faces are depicted in this how-to book. Youngsters can easily follow the step-by-step photographs to achieve the looks they want in time steps. Using watercolors and makeup sponges and brushes, children will be able to turn themselves into teddy bears for the teddy bear picnic, ghosts, monsters, or seven other creatures. No precautions are given about extra care around the eyes, so if you use this book remember to tell children to be extra careful about applying watercolor around the eye area.

Truman, Ron. *Makeup Art*. Franklin Watts, 1991. 48p. (I)
   A lot of creative ideas for designing unusual faces are illustrated by color photographs. Step-by-step directions from sketch to finished face show the reader how to create unusual faces. The emphasis is more on theatrical characters than unusual children's party faces. Helpful hints, such as wearing headbands and sitting the model on a raised seat, are provided. No safety precautions are given. An extensive materials list is provided along with names and addresses of suppliers.

9

FISHING

Fishing can get a student hooked on careers such as a marine biologist, fish hatchery worker, naturalist, fish farmer, ichthyologist, commercial fisherman, guide, ecologist, and conservationist.

Skills that fishing engenders include problem solving, strategizing, how to read a stream, patience, timing, and how to attach a worm to a hook.

Luenn, Nancy. *Nessa's Fish*. Atheneum, 1990. Unpaged. Illustrated by Neil Waldman. (P)

In the Arctic tundra, Nessa and her grandmother make a good catch of fish and store them in a stone cache. Unfortunately, grandmother becomes ill leaving Nessa to guard both her and the fish from a fox, wolves, and a brown bear. She bravely and cleverly staves off all poachers until the family comes to rescue them. Neil Waldman's vivid illustrations echo the palette of the tundra.

HOBBY STARTER ACTIVITY

▪ *Master/Apprentice Fishing School*

Fishing is one of those activities learned best with one-on-one instruction from a master fisherman. So reach out to community members who not only fish but who also would be willing to meet together with your group, preferably at a good fishing spot, to provide an introduction to fishing. Contacts may be found through your local Rod and Gun Club or the local group of the American Bass Association. Each is committed to assisting youth learn to fish.

LANGUAGE ARTS ACTIVITY

◼ *Fish Sandwich Books*

Have the boys and girls select a fish to investigate. Make available nonfiction books, encyclopedias, pamphlets, Internet connections, and other resources. Have the children write up short reports about their fish on fish-shaped sheets of paper. Construct fish-shaped front and back covers from construction paper. Display the books on a bulletin board that features an underwater background.

POEM

Bourinot, Arthur S. "Fish." In *Read Aloud Rhymes for the Very Young* selected by Jack Prelutsky. Alfred A. Knopf, 1986. Illustrated by Marc Brown.

VOCABULARY GROWTH WORDS

Angler: A fisherman who uses just a hook and line.

Artificial lure: A gadget made of wood, metal, fur, or feathers used to attract fish.

Creel: A container for holding fish after they are caught. Usually it is a wicker basket or a canvas bag.

Drag: The brake on a fishing reel.

Eddy: A spot in the stream where the flow curves back upstream.

Fly: A fishing lure composed of a hook, fur, and feathers intended to resemble an insect.

Jig: A fishing lure that has a lead head that is jiggled up and down in the water.

Plug: A wooden artificial lure that is carved to look like a fish.

Strike: A sudden fish bite on the lure.

Weight: A lead ball used to sink the fishing line.

RESOURCES

Bass Anglers Sportsman Society
P.O. Box 1716
Montgomery, AL 36141-0116
http://www.bassmaster.com

This group of fishing enthusiasts has an outreach program for children titled BASSMASTER CastingKids. Local B.A.S.S. groups sponsor competitions for boys and girls during which fishing skills are fostered.

READ MORE ABOUT IT

Arnosky, Jim. *Crinkleroot's 24 Fish Every Child Should Know*. Bradbury Press, 1993. Unpaged. (P)
    This book includes freshwater and saltwater species illustrated in watercolors. Each is clearly labeled. That is it; a good book for the very young naturalist.

Arnosky, Jim. *Fish in a Flash! A Personal Guide to Spin-Fishing*. Bradbury Press, 1991. 64p. (I)
    In his storyteller manner, Arnosky retells various adventures he has had spin-fishing while at the same time provides helpful information to the young fisherperson. He focuses on spin fishing, the latest fishing method that began in Europe after World War II. The great characteristics of spin fishing are the ease, accessibility, and relative cheapness of the sport. Arnosky's book appeals to the experienced as well as the novice sportsperson.

Morey, Shaun. *Kids' Incredible Fishing Stories*. Workman, 1996. 120p. (I)
    Girls and boys retell their fish catching escapades with assistance from Shaun Morey. He sets the scenes and then hands the story over to the children. The children tell amazing tales that include stories of catching fish that outweigh their catchers, of a little three-year-old girl catching a four-pound trout, of hooking and reeling in a stolen bike, and of an eight-year-old boy catching a world record steelhead. Morey's lively writing style keeps the action and humor moving briskly along. An added attraction is his addition of fish facts in side bar boxes.

Rosen, Michael J. *The Kids' Book of Fishing*. Workman, 1991. 96p. (I)
    A well-supplied tackle box accompanies this book about fishing. It is full of helpful hints on how to bait the hook, read the water, and tie knots as well as how to get the fish to bite and what to do when it does. The many illustrations make the directions easy to follow.

Whieldon, Tony. *Fishing*. Random House, 1994. 76p. (I)
    The tools, equipment, and techniques related to the hobby of fishing are described in a scrapbook format. Sections are devoted to specific kinds of fishing: freshwater, saltwater, river, bank, and boat. Information is provided about bait, knot tying, and rods and reels. Whieldon, a British writer, gives the young reader a credible introduction to fishing. Angler's hints are scattered throughout the text. Varieties of fish are displayed on the end papers.

10
HORSES

A love for horses leads to skill in riding, which leads to athleticism, coordination, a sense of balance, communication between child and horse, avoidance of being kicked, bitten, or thrown off, care and handling of the horse, mucking out the stable, and good sportsmanship.

Careers that result from an interest in an equestrian lifestyle include horse racing, rodeo work, equine therapy, veterinarian work, horse show managing, farm and ranch work, and horse breeding.

Van Camp, Richard. *What's the Most Beautiful Thing You Know About Horses?* Children's Book Press, 1998. Unpaged. Illustrated by George Littlechild. (P–I)

Bold and brilliant illustrations by Canadian artist George Littlechild complement the question-and-answer text by Richard Van Camp. Set in the Northwest Territories of Canada where there are no horses, the question, "What's the Most Beautiful Thing You Know About Horses?" inspires a series of imaginative responses from family and friends. The illustrations are as fanciful as the answers. This imaginative book by these commended native Canadians will elicit language arts and art activities.

HOBBY STARTER ACTIVITY

▪ *Adopt a Horse*

Owning and caring for a horse is an expensive proposition. In lieu of actual horse ownership, locate a horse within walking or carpooling distance from your location. With the owner's help and permission, have your group visit the horse periodically and perform the following horse-care skills: properly feed the horse an apple or carrot, clean the horse's hooves, curry the horse's mane and tail with a curry comb, walk the horse, put on a halter and lead, saddle the horse properly, muck out the stall, and distribute fresh straw.

LANGUAGE ARTS ACTIVITY

■ *Survey*

Following the question posed by the author of the book, Richard Van Camp, have your students survey their friends, family, and neighbors to discover what people think is the most beautiful thing about horses. Have each child draw a crayon illustration of each answer. Compile the illustrations and answers into a group book.

POEM

Hubbell, Patricia. *A Grass Green Gallop*. Atheneum, 1990. Illustrated by Ronald Himler.
Select any poem to read aloud to your group.

VOCABULARY GROWTH WORDS

Bit: In this context, a bit is a metal device attached to the reins and placed in the horse's mouth.

Colt: A young male horse.

Cross-country: A riding/jumping course set around a rural area.

Filly: A young female horse.

Gait: The manner in which a horse moves its legs.

Hands: The traditional way to measure a horse's height. One hand equals four inches.

Mare: A female horse.

Stallion: A male horse used for breeding.

Tack: The equipment needed to ride a horse, including reins, bridle, saddle, halter, and lead.

Withers: The top of the horse's shoulders.

RESOURCES

United States Pony Clubs (USPC)
4041 Iron Works Pike
Lexington, KY 40511-8462
http://www.ponyclub.org

According to the USPC Web site, "This organization promotes opportunities for instruction and competition in English riding, horse sports, and horse management for children and young adults up to 21 years of age." The Web site includes news, games, a bookstore, and links to USPC clubs, equestrian organizations, and publications.

READ MORE ABOUT IT

McFarland, Cynthia. *Hoofbeats: The Story of a Thoroughbred*. Atheneum, 1993. Unpaged. (P–I)

Originally a Thoroughbred was a cross between Arabian stallions and British mares. Now established as a breed of racehorses, their breeding and care are carefully monitored. In this photo essay about Thoroughbreds, readers discover the facts about Thoroughbred care, feeding, and training through the life of Sailor. His life is depicted from birth to training to his first race. Young horse lovers will enjoy learning about the magnificent breed by reading McFarland's book.

Meltzer, Milton. *Hold Your Horses: A Feedbag Full of Fact and Fable*. HarperCollins, 1995. 133p. (I)

Hooray! Prizewinning author and child-adored subject meet in this book. Milton Meltzer does here what he does best, contextualizing a topic within history. He has done it with gold and potatoes and now he does the same with horses. In his lively writing style, Meltzer recounts the historical and cultural context of horses as well as their contributions to war, work, and sport. He reminds his readers of horses' value, both monetarily and in socioeconomic status. As the old Irish minstrel song goes, "Three glories of a gathering are: a beautiful wife, a good horse and a swift hound." Meltzer makes a special effort to highlight horsewomen as jockeys, mounted police, and ranchers. Archival photographs and drawings are interspersed throughout the text.

Patent, Dorothy Hinshaw. *Quarter Horses*. Holiday House, 1985. 91p. Photographs by William Muñoz. (I)

Trusted nonfiction writer, Dorothy Hinshaw Patent has written a book that tells young readers everything they would want to know about quarter horses. These well-muscled animals are an American product bred for their speed and agility. Earliest known in pre-colonial Virginia, the quarter horse is respected as a speedy racehorse, a gentle family riding horse, and a cattle-working horse. Muñoz's black-and-white photographs enhance the text.

Peterson, Cris. *Horsepower: The Wonder of Draft Horses*. Boyds Mill Press, 1997. 32p. Photographs by Alvis Upitis. (P)

    Built for power not for speed, draft horses have plowed our fields, brought milk and groceries to the city, and transported people to their destinations. This photo essay relates the contributions that Percherons, Clydesdales, and Belgians, the three major breeds of draft horses, have made. How the horses are trained for shows and field days is described. We learn the definition of horsepower: the amount of energy it takes to pull 150 pounds out of a 220-foot hole in one minute.

Pritchard, Louise. *My Pony Book*. DK, 1998. 61p. (P–I)

    This how-to book will give the young equestrian information about pony care and riding techniques. In DK's distinctive format, the text is not overwhelming for the young reader. Primarily illustrated with color photographs and with each topic limited to two pages, the book is a sure magnet to the young reader dreaming of owning a pony.

11

INSECTS

Entomology aids in the development of a child's powers of observation, identification, classification, and categorization skills, knowledge of life cycles, and patience. Knowing about insects, their habits, and habitats leads to an understanding of the interrelationships between insects, other animals, plants, and the environment. To understand the needs of a butterfly is to understand the needs of all living things.

An interest in insects can lead to careers in environmental science, agriculture, professional entomologist, teaching, conservation, and social sciences.

Fancher, Lou. *The Quest for the One Big Thing*. Disney Press, 1998. Unpaged. Illustrated by Lou Fancher. (P–I)

In this counting book, an ant named Dot wants to get the big sticky thing back to her ant colony. All by herself she fails, but day after day she enlists more and more help. Teamwork wins the day. Twelve insects working together reach the goal.

HOBBY STARTER ACTIVITY

▣ *Insect Zoo*

Materials

Flowerpot
Small glass bottle, such as an olive bottle
Clear plastic soda bottle (the two-liter size; cut open at both ends)
Water
Twigs and leaves
Cheesecloth
Rubber band
Soil

Directions

1. Fill the flowerpot with soil.
2. Fill the small glass bottle with water up to about the one-third level.
3. In the bottle place grass or leafy twigs from the type of plant a specific insect eats.
4. Center and insert the small glass bottle into the soil.
5. Plunge one end of the plastic bottle into the soil so that the glass bottle is inside of it.
6. Cover the other end of the plastic bottle with cheesecloth.
7. Secure the cheesecloth with a rubber band.
8. Now your zoo is ready for inhabitants. It is time to go on a bug hunt.

▪ *Going on a Bug Hunt*

During the summer take a walk with a flashlight at nighttime in order to find some of the insects in this chart.

Insect	Location
Dragonflies	On plant stalks
Katydids	In tall grass
Black crickets	On the lawn
Daddy longlegs	On the lawn
Moths	Near outdoor lights
Tree crickets	On tree trunks
Beetles	On plant leaves

LANGUAGE ARTS ACTIVITY

▪ *I-Shaped Paragraphs*

Materials

Paper (8½" x 11") cut into the shape of the capital letter "I." Be certain that the top and bottom of the "I" are wide enough to accommodate a full sentence.

Construction paper (8½" x 11") cut into the shape of the capital letter "I" (two pieces; one for the front and one for the back)

Stapler and staples

Directions

1. Have your group study one of the insects on their charts.
2. After they have compiled a body of facts about an insect, have them come up with an umbrella sentence for the first sentence.
3. On the paper, have this sentence written on the top bar of the "I."
4. Have the children write three related, detail-type sentences under the umbrella sentence. These sentences go on the upright column of the "I."
5. Have them end their paragraph with the first sentence repeated and written on the bottom bar of the "I."
6. Have the children assemble their books by aligning the covers and pages. Staple at the top.

Example

Ants are very active insects.

    They scurry about

    looking for food.

    Some ants build

    anthills for shelter.

    Other ants take

    care of ant eggs.

Ants are very active insects.

POEM

Rossetti, Christina. "The Caterpillar." In *Sing a Song of Popcorn* selected by Beatrice Schenk de Regniers, Eva Moore, Mary Michaels White, and Jan Carr. Scholastic, 1988.

Florian, Douglas. *Insectlopedia*. Harcourt Brace Jovanovich, 1998.

VOCABULARY GROWTH WORDS

Abdomen: The posterior part of an insect's body.

Ant: An insect generally wingless that lives in complex colonies; a member of the Formicidae family.

Antenna: A pair of jointed insect parts that is used as a sensory organ.

Beetle: A large insect family that is characterized by a chewing mouthpart and two hard front wings that cover membranous back wings.

Butterfly: An insect with a slender body and four often brightly colored patterned wings.

Entomologist: A person who formally studies insects in a scientific manner.

Exoskeleton: The hard outside shell of an insect.

Grasshopper: Plant-eating insect with hind legs constructed for leaping.

Insect: A class of arthropod animals that have three pairs of jointed legs, two pairs of wings, and three body parts: head, thorax, and abdomen.

Thorax: The part of an insect between the head and the abdomen to which the six legs are attached.

RESOURCES

Amateur Entomologists' Society Bug Club
P.O. Box 8774
London, SW7 5ZG
http://www.ex.ac.uk/bugclub

   This group is part of the AES, a registered charity run by volunteers for those with an interest in entomology. The Web site includes links to bug identifications and an education section.

READ MORE ABOUT IT

Facklam, Margery. *The Big Bug Book.* Little, Brown, 1994. 32p. Illustrated by Paul Facklam. (P)
   This well-organized text starts with the basic facts about insects including a clear diagram of the parts. It moves on to describing twelve insects that are known for their large size. Interesting facts are given in a smoothly written, sensible narrative. The illustrations are drawn in the actual size of each insect.

Jenkins, Martin. *Wings, Stings, and Wriggly Things.* Candlewick Press, 1996. 24p. (P)
   Although this picture book includes snails, earthworms, and spiders, it is primarily about insects. It is a compendium of zany, yet accurate illustrations of insects along with interesting facts about each. For children who enjoy the insect coupled with scientific accuracy, this is a captivating book. Information is divided into tidbits, so there is nothing overwhelming. It would be a neat book for the unmotivated, underachieving reader, as well as the younger, gifted reader.

Llewellyn, Claire. *I Didn't Know That Some Bugs Glow in the Dark.* Copper Beech Books, 1997. 32p. Illustrated by Mike Taylor, Rob Shone, and Jo Moore. (P)
   Colorful illustrations set against a black background draw the reader into this amazing fact book. Readers are advised to read the introduction because it tells how to make the best use of the book: symbols to look for, the true/false set of questions, and the borders for more amazing facts. Each couple of pages begins with "I didn't know that" and proceeds with an exposition about that amazing fact. An even dozen rounds out the collection of facts.

Merrick, Patrick. *Dragonflies.* The Child's World, 1998. 32p. (P)
   "Cool!" will be the reaction children will have to the close-up full-color photographs. Dragonflies in the various stages of their life cycle are portrayed. Plenty of dragonfly information is compressed into the text suitable for the primary age child.

Rosenblatt, Lynn. *Monarch Magic.* Williamson Publishing, 1999. 96p. (P–I)
   Photographs of children being intensely involved with butterfly culture help make this book a must-read for children. Rosenblatt, an experienced elementary school teacher, describes more than 40 activities. Science, craft, and language arts activities round out the text.

12

JEWELRY MAKING

Today's child playing around with lacing pony beads into zipper pulls may lead to tomorrow's professional jewelry designer. Skills that derive from jewelry making include fine motor coordination; perception of design; and an understanding of the elements and principles of design (shape, line, pattern, color, space, and arrangement). Manual dexterity and a sense of what is visually pleasing are acquired as children make a piece of jewelry. Creating adornment is a worldwide interest. Every culture puts its unique stamp on jewelry design. An appreciation of the diversity and the variety of design contributed by many cultures will result from a jewelry-making hobby.

Careers that may develop from an interest in jewelry are gemologist, jewelry designer, anthropologist, folk art museum curator, occupational therapist, art therapist, recreational worker, researcher, and dental and medical appliance designer. Like all hobbies, jewelry making gives children an advantage and makes their lives more interesting. It provides children with a skill that may be shared with others, thus opening up opportunities to make new friends.

Reid, Margarette S. *A String of Beads*. Dutton Children's Books, 1997. Unpaged. Illustrated by Ashley Wolff. (P–I)

Ashley Wolff's illustrations, made even more striking and colorful with black backgrounds, support Reid's story line. A little girl tells us all about beads as she strings a necklace together with Grandma's help. Grandma tells her granddaughter the history, lore, and function of beads in many cultures. At the book's end, the author includes an interesting facts section. Of course the book lends itself to a necklace construction activity but sorting and categorization activities would also be a natural follow-up.

54 ■ *12—JEWELRY MAKING*

HOBBY STARTER ACTIVITY

▪ *Zipper Pull*

Materials

Small key ring
1 cord, about 7 inches long (3-ply, nylon braided cord is suggested)
9 pony beads in one color or various colors

Directions

1. Find the halfway point in the cord and make a loop.
2. Using a lark's head knot, attach the looped cord to the key ring. In other words, push the loop through the key ring. Pull the ends of the cord through the loop and pull tight.
3. Loosely weave the beads by stringing in an alternate manner the two ends of the cord back and forth through each set of two to three beads (see Figure 12.1).
4. Tie off with a square knot.

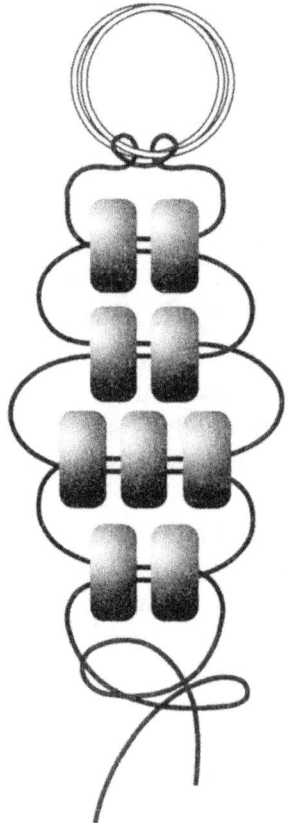

Figure 12.1. Zipper pull.

LANGUAGE ARTS ACTIVITY

▪ *Demonstration Speech*

Materials

Large beads with holes large enough for a shoelace to go through
Shoelaces
Key rings

Have your students show younger children how to make a zipper pull or other accessory. Use large beads and shoelaces so small hands can be successful. Help your group work out a step-by-step presentation.

Have them tell you what to do. Be sure not to do a step without being told, so they come to know giving directions requires a thorough think-through of each step, plus repetition. After a few rehearsals have them teach younger children.

POEM

Bryan, Ashley. "Beaded Braids." In *Sing to the Sun: Poems and Pictures by Ashley Bryan*. HarperCollins, 1992.

VOCABULARY GROWTH WORDS

Bracelet: A decorative band worn around the wrist.

Brooch: A large decorative pin.

Chatelaine: An ornamental, oftentimes useful and decorative clasp, container, or pocket hung from a belt; it was used by seamstresses, nurses, librarians, and teachers to hold the small tools of their trade. Originally, the word referred to the woman who held the keys to the rooms of a chateau.

Filigree: A decoration of fine twisted or braided wire.

Findings: The attachments for jewelry such as an earring hook or the pin part of a brooch.

Lanyard: A braided cord or rope used to fasten one item to another.

Lapidary: The craft of creating jewelry from gemstones.

Pendant: The decorative object hanging from a chain or earring such as a locket.

Ornament: Anything that decorates.

Torque: A type of open necklace.

RESOURCES

The Bead Museum
5754 West Glenn Drive
Glendale, AZ 85301
http://www.thebeadmuseum.com

    The Bead Museum in Glendale, Arizona houses one of the world's largest collections of beads. According to the museum, its purpose is to "collect and preserve, document and display beads and ornaments used in personal adornment from ancient, ethnic, and contemporary cultures, covering all periods of history." It sponsors exhibits, special events, and classes. The Web site provides information about the exhibits, schedule of classes, and descriptions of events.

READ MORE ABOUT IT

Doney, Meryl. *Jewelry*. Franklin Watts, 1996. 32p. (P–I)

    Part of the World Crafts series, this book is a perfect companion to *A String of Beads*. In clear and simple step-by-step language, the directions for making a variety of necklaces are given. Using no more than seven steps, young jewelers and their friends can put together a necklace based upon a specific culture. Cultures included are Italy, India, New Guinea, Morocco, South Africa, South America, and China. The multicultural nature of jewelry is emphasized as it is in many jewelry hobby books. Directions for two useful jewelry-making accessories, a display board and a bead-threading tray, are provided on the last two pages.

Gayle, Katie. *Snappy, Jazzy Jewelry*. Sterling, 1995. 46p. (P–I)

    A book that lives up to its title, it shows children how to make appealing jewelry. Snappy, jazzy photographs are sure to inspire the young jewelry maker and to provide many stimulating ideas. The author supplies safety tips, lists of materials, and techniques. Gayle then launches into the directions for making jewelry pieces. Katie Gayle knows how to write directions that are easily followed.

Robson, Denny. *Jewelry*. Gloucester Press, 1993. 32p. (P–I)

    Many different types of materials and jewelry are featured in Robson's book. Pastry, papier-mâché, wire, paper, and yarn are employed to make pom-poms, necklaces, torques, pins, hair ornaments, bangles, and brooches. A useful addition comes on the last page where the patterns and directions for making gift bows are given. This book is part of the Rainy Day Arts and Crafts series that also includes books about kites, masks, and puppets.

Sadler, Judy Ann. *Beading.* Kids Can Press, 1998. 40p. Illustrated by Tracy Walker. (P–I)

Bracelets, earrings, necklaces, and barrettes are all possible for the young person to create. The beads mentioned are inexpensive and easily obtainable—seed beads, bugle beads, and E beads. While most projects described do not need a loom, Sadler includes a few that do and she shows the young person how to construct a bead loom from a shoe box, 30 toothpicks, and duct tape. The easy-to-follow directions along with the clear illustrations by Tracy Walker almost guarantee the successful completion of a piece of jewelry that the young jeweler will be proud to show off to friends.

Tythacott, Louise. *Jewelry.* Thomson Learning, 1995. 48p. (I)

Anthropologist Louise Tythacott takes the reader on a round-the-world tour of jewelry. As we travel along, she points out, for different ethnic groups, the importance of jewelry, its uses, and the various materials used to create it. A world map is colored to indicate the region visited in each section. Directions for making simple jewelry are provided intermittently. Part of the Traditions Around the World series, it is intended to help readers see life from a multicultural point of view.

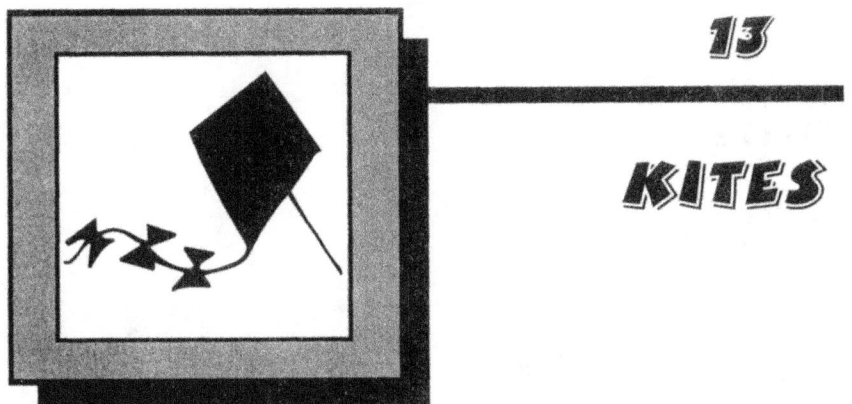

13 KITES

Soaring on an interest borne upon the thrill of flying kites, boys and girls will gain skill in understanding the principles of aerodynamics, beginning steps in aeronautical engineering, artistic design, knot tying, and kite construction. Kite construction and flying is a hobby enjoyed by boys and girls in many cultures. Each culture has its own distinctive kite designs and folklore associated with this hobby. Children will come to know that there isn't just one way to construct a kite. As with many hobbies, opportunities to study, compare, and contrast many cultures abound.

Mayer, Mercer. *Shibumi and the Kitemaker*. Marshall Cavendish, 1999. Unpaged. Illustrated by Mercer Mayer. (P–I)

Mercer Mayer pays homage to his years of appreciation of Japanese culture in his most recent book in which he tells the tale of a bargain made by an emperor's daughter. Shibumi, the emperor's daughter is so distraught by the suffering that exists in the city that surrounds her father's palace that she calls for the royal kitemaker to make her a gigantic kite. At first the kitemaker does not succeed in making a big enough kite to satisfy Shibumi, but at last he does. He then asks her what the purpose of the kite will be. She replies that the kite will end the suffering in the city. With the assistance of the kitemaker, she is attached to the kite and flies high above the city much to the despair of her parents. She makes a bargain with her father that she will come down only after he has made the city as beautiful as the palace. He agrees to the bargain only to have his greedy nobles conspire against him. At this point, the kitemaker and the emperor's daughter fly far away and disappear for years. After much time passes, a young samurai sets out to find and bring back the daughter so that she can see that her father has fulfilled his part of the bargain. Mayer's exquisite, authentically detailed illustrations portray a Japanese fantasy kingdom in which good overcomes evil.

HOBBY STARTER ACTIVITY

▪ *Garbage Bag Kites*

Materials

A light-colored garbage bag	Glue
Stickers	Plastic or wire ring
String (or fishing line)	Tagboard
Markers	

Directions

1. Lay out the garbage bags on a flat surface.
2. With the marker, draw the outline of a fish on it so that the bottom of the fish is along a folded side of the garbage bag (see Figure 13.1A).
3. Cut out the fish shape being careful not to cut at the fold line.
4. Unfold the garbage bag fish.
5. Glue a one-inch-wide strip of tagboard at the edge of the fish's mouth (see Figure 13.1B).
6. Glue the edges of the kite except for the fish's mouth.
7. Refold the kite leaving the mouth open and being sure that the edge is well-glued together.
8. Attach string or fishing line to the edges of the fish's mouth (see Figure 13.1C).
9. Knot the ends so the string does not slip out of the tagboard.
10. Attach the other ends to a lightweight plastic or wire ring.
11. Attach a very long string to the ring.
12. Decorate the kite with stickers.
13. Find an area free from electricity wires and fly your kites on a breezy day.

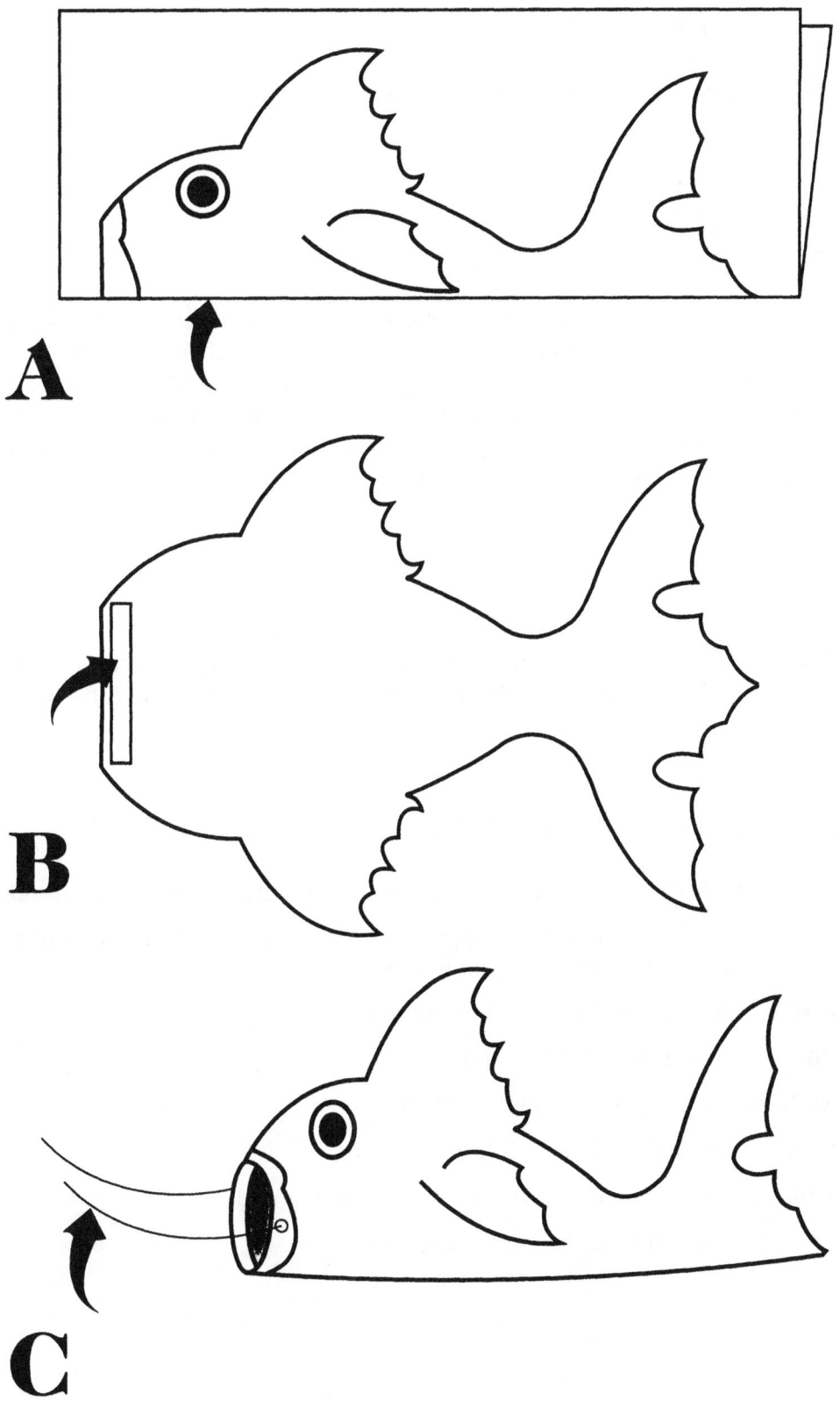

Figure 13.1. Fish kite.

LANGUAGE ARTS ACTIVITY

▪ *Videotape: You Learned It, Now Teach It*

Materials

Camcorder

Blank videotapes

Discuss and list the steps for making a kite with your group. Discuss which steps could be videotaped with which group member. Get everyone involved. Have the group prepare explanatory signs to be shown throughout the video. Help your group write a script and videotape your group presenting the directions for how to make a kite. Arrange to have it shown to another group to find out if that group can make a kite from the directions given.

POEM

Moore, Lilian. "To a Red Kite." In *Sing a Song of Popcorn* selected by Beatrice Schenk de Regniers, Eva Moore, Mary Michaels White, and Jan Carr. Scholastic, 1988.

VOCABULARY GROWTH WORDS

Airfoil: A lift-producing surface that has a curved upper part and a less curved undersurface.

Bridling: A kite-flying maneuver in which the kite flyer adjusts the angle that the kite flies to allow for wind conditions.

Flying Line: A long length of line wound on reel.

Pitch: Rotation around the lateral areas.

Roll: Rotation along the length of the kite.

Spar: A crosspiece of the kite frame.

Tail: A long streamer attached to the kite's lower end.

Yaw: Rotation around the kite's vertical axis.

RESOURCES

American Kitefliers Association (AKA)
300 North Stonestreet Avenue
Rockville, MD 20850-4117
http://www.aka.kite.org

AKA is a nonprofit organization dedicated to educating the public in the art, history, technology, and practice of building and flying kites. At this time, the Web site does not have a link to a children's page, but the organization's officials are planning one for the near future. For a complete view of what this organization has to offer, visit their Web site and review the pull-down Table of Contents.

READ MORE ABOUT IT

Caldecott, Barrie. *Kites*. Franklin Watts, 1990. 48p. (I)

Caldecott supplies the directions for the construction of six kites made of plastic sheets, Mylar, or tissue paper. These kites are not for the novice; there are up to 39 materials and tools required to make them. The kite maker should become proficient at tying knots before starting. Pictures of the required knots are provided along with an explanation of wind conditions and safety procedures.

Gibbons, Gail. *Catch the Wind: All About Kites*. Little, Brown, 1989. Unpaged. (P–I)

In Gibbons's book, Katie and Sam select, buy, and fly a kite from Ike's Kite Shop. While they choose, Ike tells them the history, types, diversity, and usefulness of this toy found in nearly every nation and culture. Directions for making a flat kite, simple and easy to follow, are given at the end of the book.

Michael, David. *Making Kites*. Kingfisher Books, 1993. 40p. (P–I)

David Michael describes how to construct nine kites. Most kites can be constructed in five to six steps. Michael breaks down what might appear complicated into easy-to-follow, step-by-step instructions. The fanciest kite described is the hexafringe kite, which takes 11 steps to make and requires adult help to do some drilling. After the easily obtained materials are gathered, a 10-year-old could put together most any one of these kites in less than an hour. An excellent feature of this book is the first 17 pages, which clearly describe kite making basics and flying hints that could be applied to all kites. Part of the Step-by-Step series, this book provides the first steps to a career in aeronautical engineering or joy-filled days flying kites.

Sams, Kenneth. *Flying Toys*. Sally Milner, 1992. 52p. (I)

Not quite kites, not quite paper airplanes, the toys described in this book are called UFOs, unconventional flying objects. Easy-to-follow, step-by-step directions are given for constructing toys that spin, glide, and fly. Children can select and make a project quickly.

Schmidt, Norman. *The Great Kite Book*. Sterling, 1997. 96p. (I)

    Not for the young child or novice kite maker, this book contains step-by-step directions for creating gorgeous, fancy kites. All the kites in the book are made from Tyvek (Dupont), which is a spunbonded polyethylene, a material that may be cut, sewn, glued, and colored. It is usually purchased in sheet form from paper supply stores. With clear diagrams in sequential order to instruct and gorgeous photographs to inspire, the author leads the kite maker through the process of making nineteen kites. The introduction contains scientific, technical, aesthetic, and philosophical information.

14

MASK CONSTRUCTION

Creating masks helps children master various craft techniques such as modeling with papier-mâché, painting, gluing, and creating designs. Mask construction engages children's imagination and creativity. The study of masks leads to an understanding of their use in many cultures. Because many cultures design masks, there are hundreds of ways to make them. Masks may be found in Africa, India, Indonesia, Japan, Australia, Micronesia, Europe, and North and South America. Masks serve religious and theatrical purposes. A mask-making hobby may lead to careers in the theater, movies, display work, television production, and big events such as carnivals and holiday parades.

Cohen, Miriam. *The Real-Skin Rubber Monster Mask.* Greenwillow Books, 1990. Unpaged. Illustrated by Lillian Hoban. (P)

Part of The First Grade Years series, this easy-to-read book tells the story of Jim and his second grade pals. Jim wants a frightening, disgusting mask. He purchases it and loves wearing it until, in the middle of trick-or-treating, he begins to feel uneasy. Is he scared of his own mask? No matter. The candy treats are abundant.

HOBBY STARTER ACTIVITY

▪ *Fantasy Masks*

Materials

Purchased inexpensive or used simple plastic masks
Newspaper
White glue
Paintbrushes
Poster paint
Gesso
Elastic band measured to fit around the head plus two inches for the knots
Cardboard

Directions

1. Anchor the mask with tape to a heavy piece of cardboard.
2. Tear the newspaper into bits (approximately one-inch squares).
3. Cover the mask with overlapping bits of newspaper.
4. Paint each piece with diluted glue as you go along.
5. Create three layers of newspaper and glue in this fashion.
6. Let it dry.
7. Add features such as warts.
8. At the sides of the masks, poke small holes for the elastic band.
9. Paint the mask with gesso.
10. Let it dry.
11. Paint the mask in whatever fashion you choose.
12. When all is ready and intact, slip one end of elastic through one of the holes leaving a long end.
13. Make a knot at the end of that long end.
14. Pull the elastic through.
15. Slip the other end through the hole on the other side of mask. Secure with a knot.

LANGUAGE ARTS ACTIVITY

▣ *A Little Theater*

Your group of children has created individual fanciful, imaginative characters. What would those characters do if they came to life? What would they say to each other?

Help your group create a short skit. Using chart paper and a marker, record their script. Prompt them with such questions as:

What would happen if _____?

Then what would happen?

How would _____ react to that?

What would _____ say?

How would _____ answer?

Then what?

POEM

Merriam, Eve. "Mask." In *Halloween ABC*. Macmillan, 1987. Illustrated by Lane Smith.

VOCABULARY GROWTH WORDS

Half-mask: A mask covering the upper part of the face.

Harlequin: A character in a comedy that wears a mask and a distinctive multicolor diamond patterned costume.

Impersonation: To act like a particular person.

Masquerade: A gathering of people wearing masks and dancing; a masked ball.

Mummery: Playful merrymaking at Christmas when people put on masks to celebrate.

No mask: A mask worn in a Japanese drama. They are often carved of wood. Most have no facial expression.

Papier-mâché: A moldable substance made from paper pulp and a seizing agent. It air dries to create a hard shell.

Proportion: The symmetrical distribution of parts to achieve balance.

Theatrical mask: A mask created specifically for a character in a play, musical, or operatic production.

RESOURCES

Masks.org
P.O. Box 12089
Olympia, WA 98508
http://www.masks.org

Masks.org is a single-subject research library serving the global community. It archives mask images and works with museums and libraries to promote and improve public understanding of diverse world cultures. Children are encouraged to contribute pictures of masks created by children for display in the Mask.org art gallery.

READ MORE ABOUT IT

Doney, Meryl. *Masks*. Franklin Watts, 1995. 32p. (P–I)

A terrific how-to book! A satisfactory product is sure to result by following the author's easy-to-follow directions. Bright attractive photographs show and inspire children to create masks on their own. If adult help is needed, an icon indicates such. The multicultural theme includes masks from India, Mexico, Nigeria, and China. Other books in the Franklin Watts World Crafts series include *Puppets*, *Toys*, and *Musical Instruments*.

Flanagan, Alice. *Masks!* Children's Press, 1996. 32p. (P–I)

Attractive clear photographs illustrate the major point of this book: masks have many uses and significances depending on the time and culture. Burial masks from Peru, a welder's protective mask, festival masks from Spain or Seneca, corn husk masks, and mud masks from New Guinea are only a few of the many masks shown. Masks tell the observer much about the culture. A glossary is included.

Gelber, Carol. *Masks Tell Stories*. Millbrook Press, 1993. 71p. (I)

Masks serve a variety of purposes in many cultures. For adults looking for ways to infuse diversity and cultural awareness into the activities for their groups, this is a helpful book. Curing sickness, maintaining law and order, warding away evil spirits from a bride, and celebrating holidays have been traditional uses of masks. More contemporary uses include sports protection such as the ice hockey goalie mask, and protective masks such as hospital masks and scuba divers' safety masks. In all cultures around the world people use masks.

McNiven, Helen, and Peter McNiven. *Making Masks*. Thomson Learning, 1995. 32p. (P–I)

Directions for creating 10 full-face masks made from a variety of materials are presented. Papier-mâché, torn paper mosaics, and dough are just a few of the materials used. Two pages are dedicated to each variety. The McNivens describe how to create a Chinese dragon, wild beasts, and pecking birds. A glossary is included.

Wright, Lyndie. *Masks*. Franklin Watts, 1990. 48p. (P–I)

One disappointment that new mask makers often have is that the facial features of the finished masks are out of proportion. Wright takes care of this problem by explaining facial proportion. She provides a lined guide showing where the nose, eyes, and mouth need to go. Directions for making paper plate masks, flat cardboard masks, bird masks, papier-mâché masks, balloon masks, and plastic container masks are given. Wright tells the reader how to make a great robot mask that would be a winner at the next play or Halloween event. She emphasizes fun, easy-to-make masks created from recycled stuff around the house. Useful and informational additions include how to fasten masks, further information, and a history of masks.

15

MUSIC

Everyone enjoys music at several levels throughout their lifetime. Whether half listening to background music or fully involved in appreciating an operatic solo, we resonate to music's magic. A music hobby encourages children's first steps toward becoming choir members, performers, commentators, ethnomusicologists, musical instrument makers, audience members, band members, music historians, agents, impresarios, choral conductors, or disc jockeys among others.

This hobby develops skills in recognizing and using pitch, rhythm, melody, harmony, and a sense of what is musically pleasing.

The multicultural qualities of music provide a chance to appreciate the world's diversity and the thousands of songs to be heard and sung.

Isadora, Rachel. *Ben's Trumpet*. Greenwillow Books, 1979. Unpaged. Illustrated by Rachel Isadora. (P)

Isadora's striking illustrations capture the jazzy rhythms of the musicians who play at the Zig Zag Jazz Club. Ben listens longingly to the music emanating from the Zig Zag Jazz Club. He watches the musicians and plays his imaginary trumpet. Finally, the trumpeter who sees Ben's desire to be a musician notices him. The last illustration is in marked contrast to the rest of the book and underscores the resolution of Ben's longing.

HOBBY STARTER ACTIVITY

▪ *Construct a Handbell*

Materials

Terra-cotta flowerpot
Wooden bead
Wooden dowel
Scissors
Cord (not string)
Colored tape

Directions

1. Push the cord through the bead.
2. Tie a big fat knot at the bottom of the bead so it can't slip off. That's the clapper.
3. Leave enough loose cord between the bead and the drainage hole of the flowerpot so that the clapper hits the sides of the pot.
4. Tape the remainder of the cord to the wooden dowel by winding the tape around and around the dowel and the cord.
5. At the clapper end of the dowel, wind the tape around and around the end until it is wider than the small hole in the pot.
6. Push the dowel through the drainage hole of the pot. This is the bell handle.
7. Make the handle secure in the hole. One way to do this is to wind rubber bands around and around the dowel and then tamp them down into the hole until the handle is steady and secure.
8. Decorate your handbell.

LANGUAGE ARTS ACTIVITY

▪ *Syncopated Silliness*

Get everybody into a good mood by mixing silly, fanciful poems with peppy, syncopated jazz or rock and roll music. Have your group members search your local library for silly poems with a lot of rhythm. An example is *Polka Bats and Octopus Slacks* by Caleb Brown.

Have your students sample many instrumental arrangements of rock and roll, jazz, or rhythm and blues and choose music to use in the background while the poems are read aloud. An example is *Rock Instrumental Classics*, Rhino Records. Share your group's creative combinations by putting on a program for another group.

POEM

Silverstein, Shel. "Rock 'n' Roll Band." In *Imaginary Gardens* edited by Charles Sullivan. Harry N. Abrams, 1989.

Cole, William. "Here Comes the Band." In *Sing a Song of Popcorn* selected by Beatrice Schenk de Regniers, Eva Moore, Mary Michaels White, and Jan Carr. Scholastic, 1988.

VOCABULARY GROWTH WORDS

Adagio: Slow, graceful tempo.

Allegro: Fast, brisk, or lively tempo.

Jazz: A type of music that originated in America and is characterized by syncopation, melody, and colorful orchestration.

Legato: Smooth, connected music with no break between tones, like a flowing river.

Percussion instrument: Any instrument in which the tone is made by striking, as with a xylophone or a drum.

Pitch: In music, the tone that is determined by the frequency of the sound wave vibrations.

Rhythm: The grouping of tones by accent and time value.

Stringed instruments: A musical instrument having strings, such as a violin.

Syncopation: In rhythm, the beginning of a musical phrase on the unaccented tone and carrying the tone to the accented tone. Ragtime is a type of music that uses syncopation.

Wind instruments: A musical instrument in which the sound is made by blowing breath, as with a clarinet or a trumpet.

RESOURCES

The Children's Music Network
P.O. Box 1341
Evanston, IL 60204-1341
847-733-8003
http://www.cmnonline.org

This nonprofit organization has members throughout the United States and Canada. Members consider children's music "a powerful means of encouraging cooperation, celebrating diversity, building self-esteem, promoting respect and responsibility for our environment, and cultivating an understanding of nonviolence and social justice." The Web site includes links to information about events and resources that fulfill the organization's mission.

READ MORE ABOUT IT

Ardley, Neil. *Music*. Eyewitness Books. Alfred A. Knopf, 1989. 64p. (P–I)

In the attractive style of Eyewitness Books, two pages are allotted to each instrument. The history, evolution, and construction of musical instruments are described. Concepts and terms are clearly defined and illustrated so that young readers will come away ready to converse about music and musical instruments.

deBeer, Sara, ed. *Open Ears: Music Adventures for a New Generation*. Ellipsis Kids, 1995. 141p. (I)

This is a how-to book with a twist. Sara deBeer has collected how-to directions for making musical instruments from twenty outstanding entertainers. Tom Keith of Garrison Keillor's show *A Prairie Home Companion* tells children how to create sound effects. Phoebe Snow shares her secrets of how to belt out a song. Artists show how to make and play the spoons. And on it goes. Children will be able to put together a band and entertain the neighborhood after reading this book.

Drew, Helen. *My First Music Book*. Dorling Kindersley, 1993. 48p. (P–I)

Zowie! Bright primary color photographs lure young readers into this book. Simple directions tempt kitchen-table musicians into trying their hand at constructing working musical instruments. A group of friends working for an hour can construct a jazz band and entertain their families in the afternoon. The first two pages tell how to use the directions and how to follow the book's format to make the instruments. A good balance of string, percussion, wind, and tuned percussion instruments are described. This book is fun to browse through and to imagine the possibilities and even more fun to put the pages into action.

Hart, Avery, and Paul Mantell. *Kids Make Music!: Clapping & Tapping from Bach to Rock!* Williamson, 1993. 156p. Illustrated by Loretta Trezzo Braren. (P–I)

Hurrah for the Williamson Publishing Company. It publishes children's activity books that never fail adults who are searching for ways to involve children in fun, worthwhile activities. This is no exception. Comprehensive in coverage, it discusses making music with our bodies (clapping, snapping, singing), constructing musical instruments, singing in various styles, and throwing a multicultural music party. Teach children the clapping game to accompany "Take Me Out to the Ball Game" and your trips to soccer games will never be the same. How-to directions for making musical instruments have sections as do folk music and producing shows with a multicultural flavor. Worth the price of the book is the section titled "Encore" in which the authors reveal the super secrets of musicians. You will wish that you had known these when you were 10 years old.

Oates, Eddie Herschel. *Making Music: 6 Instruments You Can Create*. HarperCollins, 1995. 32p. Illustrated by Michael Koelsch. (P–I)

The six instruments are a balloon tom-tom, a wrench xylophone, a xylodrum, a garden-hose trumpet, a spoon roarer, and a singing sitar. Each is made from commonly found household items. Clearly written directions for playing each instrument accompany the step-by-step instructions for making it.

16 POTTERY

The fun of mucking around with malleable clay to create neat (and not so neat) stuff makes this hobby popular. While we pound, form, coil, slap, design, and shape, we improve small muscle control, manual dexterity, and our notions about beauty. Pottery's multicultural qualities may cause a child to become curious about and to study other cultures. As they do, they may come to respect the many ways of potters.

Hobbyists can become ceramic designers, potters, medical and dental prosthesis designers, folk artists, sculptors, and ceramists.

Engel, Diana. *The Little Lump of Clay*. Morrow Junior Books, 1989. Unpaged. Illustrated by Diana Engel. (P)

    A little lump of clay has been repeatedly passed over by potters until a little boy takes it out of the bin. The little boy is unsuccessful in his attempts to make something of the clay and leaves it. A little girl finds the lump of clay and finally turns it into something useful, a cup for her hot chocolate. At last the lump of clay is happy, feeling special and useful.

HOBBY STARTER ACTIVITY

◼ *Greenware Pottery*

Materials

    Commercial water-based clay
    Table covering (newspaper, plastic cloth)
    An old bread board or similar item
    Tempera paint
    Varnish or shellac
    Brushes (some for varnish and others for tempera paint)
    Old towels
    Drying rack

Help your group members make an item out of a hunk of clay. Some suggestions are: a flowerpot saucer, a small flowerpot, a small bowl, a candle saucer, a soap dish, a wall vase for dried flowers, a holiday decoration, or a kitchen sink coaster for a pot scrubber.

After the item has been made, place it on a rack to dry slowly at room temperature. The more slowly it dries the less chance it has of cracking, so have the children cover their items with a damp old towel to increase drying time. Wrap unused clay in plastic and store in another plastic bag. Use up as soon as possible because it gets really yucky and smelly.

After a few days when the items are thoroughly dry, the children may decorate their items with tempera paint. When they are satisfied with the results and the paint is dry, have the children preserve the item by painting it with varnish or shellac.

LANGUAGE ARTS ACTIVITY

◼ *"Mail-Order" Catalog*

Have your students prepare a mail-order catalog for their pottery pieces. Begin by having the children study various mail-order catalogs. Have them study the order forms paying attention to the various columns: item number, item description, catalog page number, quantity, and price. Have them study the blurbs describing the items.

Take pictures of the pottery items that the children have made and have them write blurbs describing their pottery pieces. Help the children lay out the photos, blurbs, and order forms. If desired, duplicate the catalog for friends, families, and neighbors.

POEM

Clark, Ann Nolan. *The Little Indian Pottery Maker*. Melmont, 1955. Illustrated by Don Perceval.

VOCABULARY GROWTH WORDS

Earthenware: Pottery that is fired at low temperature; it is porous.

Fettle /Fettling: The act of tidying up a pottery piece after it is taken out of its mould.

Firing: Baking a pottery piece at high temperature in a special oven called a kiln.

Glaze: The glassy surface of a pottery piece created by applying a coating that melts during firing.

Greenware: Clay pottery not yet placed into the kiln.

Kiln: A special oven specifically made for pot firing.

Porcelain: Hard, white earthenware made with kaolin clay.

Stoneware: Pottery that is fired at very high temperatures; it is not porous.

Terra-cotta: A reddish-brown clay.

Throw: To form a pot on a potter's wheel.

Wedging: The process of preparing clay before using it to remove all bubbles and excessive water.

RESOURCES

Kids 'N' Clay Pottery Studio
1824 Fifth Street
Berkeley, CA 94710-1915
510-845-0982
kidsnclay@juno.com
http://www.kidsnclay.com

Children in the Bay Area may take classes at this Berkeley studio founded by Kevin Nierman. The Web site has a resource list, an activities page, and a virtual gallery of children's pottery creations. Nierman's book, *The Kids 'N' Clay Ceramics Book* may be purchased through the site as well.

READ MORE ABOUT IT

Florian, Douglas. *A Potter*. Greenwillow Books, 1991. Unpaged. (P)

In Florian's special style, the many actions that a potter takes with clay are portrayed. For example, kneading, throwing, shaping, painting with glazes, and firing are illustrated.

Gibbons, Gail. *The Pottery Place*. Harcourt Brace Jovanovich, 1987. Unpaged. (P)

    The delivery truck bounces down the country road to the pottery place and there begins the text and the day of the potter. Throughout her day, the potter goes step by step through the sequence of creating objects from clay. Technical words are explained within the text so the reader is not overwhelmed with technical language. Gibbons's pictures, warm and homey, make a complicated procedure accessible to the very young. As the potter works, a young friend comes to visit. He asks how long people have been making pots. This question gives Gibbons a chance to give a very brief history of pottery from a worldwide perspective. The steps for marketing the potter's pottery are also given in a subtle manner so that the young reader is not distracted from the story line. At the end of the book, Gibbons provides the directions for three types of pottery: pinch, coil, and slab. She writes the directions for pots made from commercially available, ready-to-use, air-dry clay so that the young potter does not need a kiln or elaborate equipment to construct a pot.

Gonen, Rivka. *Fired Up: Making Pottery in Ancient Times*. Rhinestone Press, 1993. 72p. (I)

    Illustrated primarily by black-and-white photographs, this is a serious yet readable text about the techniques that potters use from both a historical and a contemporary point of view. Uses of pottery are described. The work of archeologists and the role of scientists researching pottery from ancient times are emphasized and the universality of pottery is shown through examples from a variety of cultures.

Kohl, Mary Ann. *Mudworks*. Bright Ring Publishing, 1989. 150p. (P–I)

    Recipes for various doughs, clays, plasters, soaps, and pulps are collected in this versatile book. The emphasis is on materials; the directions for art and craft projects are minimal. Children are encouraged to follow their own inspirations. The author indicates which mixtures are more suitable for which project. For example, a zonalite concoction is used for sculpting, a flour and salt dough is used for map making, and a mix of wax and plaster of Paris is used for casting. Some mixtures are intended for pouring into moulds, others for shaping, while still others are for carving. An entire section is devoted to edible doughs including doggie biscuits.

Reid, Barbara. *Fun with Modeling Clay*. Kids Can Press, 1998. 40p. (P)

    This book gets the very young hobbyist started with skills from creating basic shapes to fanciful animals, faces and shapes, people movers, people, and buildings. The last pages describe how to create a scene with modeling clay. Cautions are listed such as getting clay off the carpet as soon as possible because it is difficult to remove once someone steps on it.

17

PUPPETS

Puppetry stimulates a child's imagination. Constructing and playing with puppets help children master oral language skills as well as design and construction abilities.

Puppetry leads to careers in teaching, theater, television production, educational television, party entertainment, occupational therapy, and speech therapy.

People around the world enjoy puppets. Learning about the puppets of other cultures will lead to an appreciation of the beauty of ethnic diversity.

Hayward, Linda. *Baker Baker Cookie Maker*. CTW, Random House, 1998. Unpaged. Illustrated by Tom Brannon. (P)

One of a series of books featuring Jim Henson's Sesame Street Muppets, this is a Step Into Reading book featuring Cookie Monster. It tells the frustrations that Cookie Monster has making cookies for all of the cookie takers and him. Not only will children get started with reading, they will also connect to a favorite *Sesame Street* puppet character.

HOBBY STARTER ACTIVITY

▪ *Puppet Stage*

Materials

Refrigerator box
Carton knife (which is extremely sharp so do not allow children to help with the cutting)
Cloth
Dowel
Cup hooks
Tempera paint
Brushes (suitable for tempera paint)

Directions

1. Obtain a refrigerator box from a furniture and appliance store.
2. Help your students construct a puppet show stage.
3. With the carton knife, cut a rectangular hole high enough from the floor for children to kneel and manipulate the puppets.
4. Help the children decorate the box with tempera paint.
5. Help them fashion a curtain by folding the edges of two pieces of cloth over the dowel and sewing in place.
6. Hang the dowel over the opening by hanging it on cup hooks that have been inserted on either side of the puppet show opening.
7. With the carton knife, cut a hole in the back of the box large enough for one child to walk through.

LANGUAGE ARTS ACTIVITY

▪ *Favorite Familiar Folktale Script*

Have your group select a favorite familiar folktale to transcribe into a puppet show script. Like reader's theater, the script could be taken from the text by eliminating the "he said," "she said" and giving the narrator all the transition and description parts. Find or make puppets and have your students put on a performance with their newly made puppet show stage.

POEM

Livingston, Myra Cohn. "The Marionettes." In *Worlds I Know and Other Poems*. Atheneum, 1985.

VOCABULARY GROWTH WORDS

Audience: An assembly of people gathered to watch and listen to a performance.

Bunraku puppet: A jointed puppet in the Japanese tradition; it resembles a marionette.

Character: Usually a person or animal in a play that acts out a part.

Glove puppet: A type of puppet that slips over the hand and that is manipulated by moving the fingers.

Marionette: A type of puppet with jointed parts attached by strings to movable wooden crosspieces.

Punch and Judy: World famous puppets. In a Punch and Judy show, the husband and wife quarrel in a silly manner.

Rod puppet: A type of puppet in which the figure is attached to dowels.

Script: The written dialogue that identifies which characters speak in what order often with directions as to how the line should be delivered.

Theater: The place where a performance occurs.

Troupe: A group of puppeteers who act and travel together.

RESOURCES

Puppeteers of America
#5 Cricklewood Path
Pasadena, CA 91107-10002
http://www.puppeteers.org

Puppeteers of America describes itself as, "A nonprofit organization that provides information about puppetry, encourages performances and builds a community of people who love puppet theater." The Web site shows the various regional guilds in the United States. A schedule of festivals, a book store, and an audiovisual library resource are provided. Users of the Web site may click on a "Consultant" button to find answers to their puppetry questions.

READ MORE ABOUT IT

Henson, Cheryl. *The Muppets Make Puppets*. Workman, 1994. 112p. (I)

Cheryl Henson and Kermit tell and show us how to make a great variety of puppets from those ubiquitous "household items." What some people have around the house is amazing. More than a craft book, it also tells how to create a voice, a character, and relationships between puppets. Directions for constructing a puppet stage are given.

Lade, Roger. *The Most Excellent Book of How to be a Puppeteer*. Copper Beech Books, 1996. 32p. Illustrated by Rob Shone. (P–I)

Lade introduces young readers to nine puppets all representing different types of puppets, for example, glove puppets, marionettes, shadow puppets, and rod puppets. Most take about 10 easy-to-follow steps to construct. The last puppet described is the Bunraku, an ancient Japanese puppetry tradition. Ideas for puppet stages are provided. Other topics in the Most Excellent series include clowns, magicians, card tricks, and juggling.

McNiven, Peter, and Helen McNiven. *Puppets*. Thomson Learning, 1995. 32p. (P–I)

The robot is a contraption constructed from household items. The ugly duckling provides a simple introduction to marionettes. The dancing troupe will have your fingers do the dancing. Other types of puppets made from easy-to-locate materials are described in this colorful book filled with clear-cut directions that do not overwhelm. Two easy pages per puppet are all it takes to tell about eleven puppets.

Watson, N. Cameron. *The Little Pigs Puppet Book*. Little, Brown, 1990. 32p. (P–I)

The little pigs write their puppet play script on their computer in this very up-to-date book on puppet making and puppet show production. Sure to delight and instruct, this book will fire up the very young readers' interest in putting on a puppet show. Step-by-step and easy-to-follow directions are provided for sock, tube, or jaw puppets as well as instructions for creating scenery, sound effects, and various types of stage construction. Refreshment recipes are provided as well as program and ticket ideas. Get ready for a neighborhood production after the children have read this delightful book.

Wright, Lyndie. *Puppets*. Franklin Watts, 1989. 48p. (P–I)

Simple directions and photographs in sequence help young puppeteers to construct various puppets. Many types of puppets are introduced: paper plate, paper bag, plastic bottle, Styrofoam ball and papier-mâché glove puppets, and more. Excellent for children in grades two through five, most of the directions are easy to follow without adult supervision. Ideas for stages are provided.

18
PUZZLES AND GAMES

The playing of games and the solving of puzzles present us with a paradox. While games and puzzles are supposed to be fun and relaxing, they require serious thinking and skill. Children who are adept at puzzles and games often grow up to be leaders and problem solvers. Often games involve negotiation and communication skills. It is the wise adult who brings a child along the path of becoming insightful into the behavior of self and others as games are played and puzzles are solved.

Ingenuity, ability to work well with others, risk taking, problem solving, strategizing, creativity, goal setting, and achieving are attributes and skills acquired in the course of playing.

Satisfying careers in recreation, the hospitality industry, entertainment, game creation, computer program designer, the sports industry, teaching, and coaching await boys and girls who just want to have fun.

Birchman, David F. *Jigsaw Jackson*. Lothrop, Lee & Shepard, 1996. Unpaged. Illustrated by Daniel San Souci. (P–I)

In this fanciful story J. J. Jackson does his best to keep busy during a long Maine winter. He plays checkers with the plow horse, reads stories to the chickens and mice, and listens to the opera with his mynah bird. J. J. Jackson is a fix-it man, and in a jiff he has the neighbor's broken clocks and harrows back in working order. Along comes Sean Shane O'Reilly McShaker, the world's greatest jigsaw puzzle maker. Now, McShaker knows a money-maker when he sees one. When he sees J. J. Jackson assemble a jigsaw puzzle instantaneously, he convinces Jackson to abandon the animals, and off they go to seek fame and fortune. But not to worry, all works out for the best in the end. San Souci's zany illustrations enliven the story.

HOBBY STARTER ACTIVITY

▪ *Have a Neighborhood Game Festival*

Materials

    4 jigsaw puzzles of the same degree of difficulty

    4 card tables

    1 tin can (approximately the size of a 1-pound can of tomatoes)

    Play area

    Hopscotch course

    Chalk

    Pebble for each child

    Large rubber ball

    Rewards for all for participating

Have your group members invite and organize the younger children in the community together for an hour of games. Discuss safety and courtesy guidelines. Have them set up four stations for playing well-known games. For example:

Station A: Red Rover

Station B: Kick the Can

Station C: Hopscotch

Station D: Spud

Have the group members divide the community children into four play groups, review the rules of each game, and play the games. After 10 minutes of playing and at a given signal, rotate the groups. Repeat until all groups have played all games.

At the end of the active play period, have a jigsaw puzzle contest. Have your group members set up four jigsaw puzzle stations. Have them invite the visiting groups to a timed contest for putting together the jigsaw puzzles. At a signal, each group works to put together their jigsaw puzzle. At the end of the 10 minutes, the group with the most pieces joined wins.

Serve refreshments. Distribute rewards and thank all for participating.

LANGUAGE ARTS ACTIVITY

▪ *Word Games*

Have the children make up games to play with their friends and families. Word games may be created by employing the following strategies:

- **Rhyming Categories**

Word Game Preparation

Think of a category such as food, pets, or sports. Create two columns on a sheet of paper. In one column list the items in the category. In the second column, list words that rhyme with each item in the first column. Create 10 of these pairs. Now you are ready to play this word puzzle.

Playing the Game

Using the prepared lists, ask your friends to tell you the name of an object in a category that rhymes with _____. For example, you might say "Tell me the name of a food that rhymes with *tickle*." Answer: pickle.

- **Rhyming Phrases**

Word Game Preparation

Think of two words that may be paired to form common phrases such as *bread and butter*. Now make a list of nonsense phrases in which other words rhyme with words in the phrase, for example, *red and clutter*. Create 10 of these phrases. Now you are ready to play the game.

Playing the Game

Reading from your prepared list, ask your friends to tell you a common phrase that rhymes with two different words. For example you might ask, "Tell me a common phrase that rhymes with *makin' and pegs*." Answer: bacon and eggs.

■ In Common

Word Game Preparation

Think up and make a list of categories: glasses, machines, windows, dolls, beans, and so on to which a modifier (adjective) could be added. List three modifiers for each category. For example, to the word *doll* the word *Barbie* or *baby* or *kewpie* could be added to make a common two- or three-word phrase. Create 10 of these. Now you are ready to play the game.

Playing the Game

Present your friends with the sets of three words (adjectives/modifiers) and ask them what word could be added after all three words to create common two- or three-word phrases. For example, you would say, "What one word would you add to *stained glass*, *picture*, or *dormer* to make common, two- or three-word phrases?" Answer: window.

POEM

Hoban, Russell. "Jigsaw Puzzle." In *A New Treasury of Children's Poetry* edited by Joanna Cole. Doubleday, 1984.

VOCABULARY GROWTH WORDS

Anagram: A competitive word game in which the players in turn form words from letters drawn from a stock of letters.

Clue: Something that helps to solve a perplexing problem.

Competition: A match or rivalry between contestants.

Conundrum: A riddle, the answer of which is a play on words called a pun.

Crossword: A type of word guessing game in which words are arranged horizontally and vertically as they are guessed from hints provided based on the words' meaning.

Fair play: Playing within the established rules of the game.

Game: A contest of physical and/or mental prowess that has established rules.

Jigsaw: A picture puzzle in which the pieces have been cut by a jigsaw.

Puzzle: A game, problem, or device invented to test one's ability to solve the problem with cleverness or skill.

Sport: A diversion that is primarily a physical game usually played on a field or court.

RESOURCES

American Jigsaw Puzzle Society
http://www.jigsaw-puzzle.org
   This group consists of enthusiasts for the jigsaw puzzle, including collectors, creators, and assemblers. Membership is free. The Web site's stated purpose is "to provide news about jigsaw puzzle events, reviews of jigsaw puzzles, and informative articles about jigsaw puzzles." It includes a history of jigsaw puzzles, a FAQ page, and links to related Web sites.

READ MORE ABOUT IT

Cole, Joanna, and Stephanie Calmenson. *Crazy Eights and Other Card Games*. Morrow Junior Books, 1994. 76p. Illustrated by Alan Tiegreen. (P–I)
   Card games galore are described here. The deck is explained as are shuffling and dealing. This is definitely a book you want to have for extended trips, rainy afternoons, or blackouts.

Cole, Joanna, and Stephanie Calmenson. *Fun on the Run: Travel Games and Songs*. Beech Tree Books, 1999. 144p. Illustrated by Alan Tiegreen. (P–I)
   This book from Beech Tree Books Activity series brings fun and games into a family's life. This time it means fun while the family is on the road. "Are we there already!" will replace "Are we there yet?" when children have this book on hand.

Editors of Klutz Press. *Kids Travel*. Klutz Press, 1994. 48p. (P–I)
   As it claims, this winner of a Parent's Choice Award is a backseat survival book. Full of games, it will keep all ages entertained as they make their way to the beach, Grandmother's, or Walt Disney World®. Packaged with it are pencils, a pair of dice, a writing board, and a tablet. You will be equipped with both ideas and materials with this ready-to-go game book.

Marchon-Arnaud, Catherine. *A Gallery of Games*. Ticknor & Fields, 1994. 57p. (I)
   In this two-for-one book, youth learn both how to construct games as well as play them. First published in France, it contains a few games that may be unfamiliar to American readers. The games are well illustrated and crafted with a polished look to them. Older boys and girls would be more likely to enjoy this collection than younger children. It would be an ideal book for a twelve-year-old looking for games to make for a younger sibling. Cutting with an X-acto knife and gluing with super glue are called for in the directions, so care needs to be taken. In addition to directions for mak-

ing and playing games, historical notes add to the interest and enjoyment of the book. Marc Schwartz's color photographs brighten up the text.

Stott, Dorothy. *The Big Book of Games*. Dalton, 1998. 64p. (P–I)

    Quick! Before video games and organized sports completely capture our children, teach them these games. These are games that children ordinarily teach to each other but just in case they have skipped a generation or two, here they are collected for you. Reading this book and sharing the contents will dust off your childhood memories. Do you remember Kick the Can or Red Light, Green Light? On a summer's evening, teach Mother, May I or Flashlight Tag. When the new snowfall arrives next winter teach them to play Buzz or Telephone or Sardines. Singing games and car trip games are also included. A fabulous resource for adults and children, this book offers the perfect antidote to that dreaded Couch Potato Syndrome.

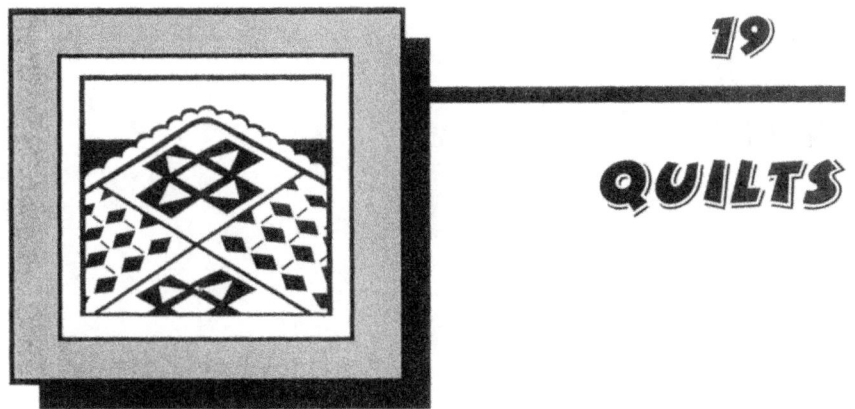

19

QUILTS

As children cut and piece together the parts of a quilt block, they improve math, measuring, and geometry skills as well as design and sewing skills. The artistic eye that notices scale, proportion, color, and pleasing arrangements develops during the process of making a quilt. When the history and story of various patterns are told, children pick up an appreciation of people's lives intertwined with quilts. Some people can tell a story in words; others can tell a story with pattern, color, and design. The young quilter may grow up to be a fashion designer, a textile designer, an interior decorator, a set designer, an engineer, a historian, or a folk art curator/appraiser.

Brumbeau, Jeff. *The Quilt Maker's Gift*. Pfeifer-Hamilton, 2000. Unpaged. Illustrated by Gail de Marcken. (P–I)

The king, an aggressively greedy man, hears that the quilt maker has not given him a gift. With legions of his soldiers in tow, he goes to the quilt maker to demand that she give him a quilt. She resists saying that she only gives her quilts to the poor, and therefore he would need to give away all his possessions. Infuriated, the king imprisons the quilt maker in a variety of ways, but she sticks to her original bargain, and the king begins to give away his treasury of gifts. As he does, he becomes happier. Each time he gives away one of his possessions, a bird messenger flies back to inform the quilt maker who would add another piece to the quilt that she is making for the king. Eventually, she seeks out the king to give him his quilt. The king and the readers of this story discover that generosity has its own reward. De Marcken's brilliantly colored illustrations are rich in detailed imagery and dazzle the reader's eye.

HOBBY STARTER ACTIVITY

▣ *Quilt Patch*

Materials

> 8" squares of plain synthetic or synthetic blend fabric (one per child; old sheets work well)
>
> Nonglossy drawing paper cut into 8" squares
>
> Scissors
>
> Fabric crayons
>
> Iron
>
> Plain fabric for lining
>
> Thread
>
> Sewing machine (optional)
>
> *Tar Beach* by Faith Ringgold

Directions

1. After reading *Tar Beach* by Faith Ringgold to your group, ask them to share what sort of fantasy being or person they would like to be and what magical powers they would like to have.
2. Tell them that they are going to design a quilt patch that depicts their fantasy.
3. Distribute the materials, giving each child an 8-inch square of drawing paper and fabric crayons.
4. Tell them to create a fantasy image of themselves by drawing a picture of their fantasy on their paper square.
5. Encourage them to think big and to use as much of the space in the 8-inch square as possible.
6. When the children have completed their drawings, help them transfer the design to the fabric.
7. On a surface prepared for ironing, have them place the cloth. On the cloth have them place the crayon drawing with the crayon side face down on top of the cloth.
8. With the iron set for cotton, have an adult iron the crayon drawing with a lift and press action in order to transfer the color onto the cloth without blurring it.
9. Turn the quilt inside out and press.
10. Turn under the edges of the open end and sew together with a blanket stitch.
11. Hang the quilt where many may admire it.

LANGUAGE ARTS ACTIVITY

▣ *Quilting Bee Discussion*

While working on quilts, people love to talk. An old-fashioned quilting bee is often a time for people to exchange experiences, to relate the news, and to share feelings.

While the children are working on their quilt squares, you have a wonderful opportunity to get children talking in a constructive, positive manner. Set up some ground rules. For example:

1. Create a climate of admiration.
2. Be sure everyone who wants to has an opportunity to speak.
3. A lively conversation is informative, pleasant, and above all, kind.
4. A good conversationalist listens actively.
5. A good conversationalist knows how to divert conversation when someone criticizes a person who is not present.
6. No talking about someone in a negative manner.

Possible topics for discussion include:

1. Tell about the funniest program you saw on television this week.
2. Who should be named the outstanding person of the month in our town? Why?
3. Tell about the best party you attended. What made it so terrific?

POEM

Piercy, Marge. "Looking at Quilts." In *Saturday's Children: Poems of Work* compiled by Helen Plotz. Greenwillow Books, 1982.

VOCABULARY GROWTH WORDS

Appliqué: Small pieces, typically used to create a picture or pattern, sewn with a zig-zag stitch, onto a larger piece of material, usually a square.

Backing: The lining of a quilt. It is usually made of tightly woven cotton or wool.

Batting: The inside lining of a quilt. It is placed, like sandwich filling between the quilt top and the backing. It makes the quilt warm and cozy.

Crazy quilt: A quilt top made by piecing together odd-shaped fabric pieces.

Frame: Usually a wooden hoop or large rectangular shaped frame that is used to keep the quilt top, batting, and backing taut while the quilting stitches are made.

Lattice strips: Long rectangular fabric strips used to create borders between quilt blocks.

Log cabin: A quilt block pattern.

Piecing: The hand- or machine-sewn joining of fabric pieces into a pattern.

Quilt block: Usually a square of fabric pieced together into geometric patterns.

Quilting: A quilt is like a sandwich consisting of the quilt top, batting, and backing. To keep these three layers together without slippage, quilters stitch the layers together with a pattern of tiny stitches. This process is called quilting.

RESOURCES

ABC Quilts
596 NH Turnpike, Suite #3
Northwood, NH 03261
http://www.mv.com/ipusers/abcquilts

ABC is an acronym for At Risk Babies Crib. Send a #10 SASE to receive information about making and sending quilts to babies who have been abandoned, are infected with HIV/AIDS, or are affected by alcohol or drugs. The Web site includes a FAQ page, pictures of quilts, and information about the book *Kids Making Quilts for Kids*, and many links to other quilting sites.

American Quilter's Society
P.O. Box 3290
Paducah, KY 43002-3290
http://www.AQSquilt.com

This organization sponsors quilting shows and contests, and they offer an appraiser certification program. The Web site provides information about events, books, and related links.

READ MORE ABOUT IT

Bial, Raymond. *With Needle and Thread*. Houghton Mifflin, 1996. 48p. (P–I)

Beautiful photographs that capture the intensity of a quilter's face or the beauty of a traditional pattern make Bial's book delightful to experience. He tells the history of American quilting and the significance of this craft to America. He quotes Cheryl Kennedy of the Illinois Documentary Quilt Project, "Quilts give women an opportunity to speak across the generations."

Cobb, Mary. *The Quilt-Block History of Pioneer Days with Projects Kids Can Make*. Millbrook Press, 1995. 64p. Illustrated by Jan Davey Ellis. (P–I)

A quiet companion book for *The Seasons Sewn* by Ann Whitford Paul, this book gives the actual templates for some of the quilts described. Directions are given for creating paper craft projects such as a recipe box, a diary, or a decorative wall hanging each based on a quilt pattern. Anecdotes about the quilt patterns are given.

Lyons, Mary E. *Stitching Stars: The Story Quilts of Harriet Powers*. Charles Scribner's Sons, 1993. 42p. (I)

Through her quilts, readers can piece together the Bible stories so important to Harriet Powers, a Georgia slave who lived during the Civil War. Appliquéd in the tradition of West Africa, these story quilts, now displayed at the Smithsonian and the Museum of Fine Arts (Boston), are remarkable for their preservation of a life, a time, and a tradition. Her second quilt is a needlework recounting of meteorological events from 1780 to 1895.

Paul, Ann Whitford. *The Seasons Sewn*. Harcourt Brace, 1996. Unpaged. Illustrated by Michael McCurdy. (I)

The reader is taken through the seasons and the stories of the quilt patterns preferred by pioneer girls and women. The careful research that the author used to discover the customs—social, medicinal, and religious—results in a fascinating recounting of pioneer life revealed by the stories behind the quilt patterns. This is a sequel to her book *Eight Hands Round*, an alphabet book based on quilt patterns.

Stalcup, Ann. *American Quilt-Making: Stories in Cloth*. PowerKids Press, 1999. 24p. (P)

Part of the Crafts of the World series, this photo essay tells the history, types, and stories of quilts. Archival black-and-white photos lend a touch of historical authenticity. Seven types of quilts are described: album, friendship, AIDS memorial, Amish, Hawaiian, Hmong, and African American. A project related to quilt making is described. Stalcup gathered a variety of full-color photographs of various quilts to document this satisfying old-yet-new hobby.

20

ROCK COLLECTING

Rocks collectors have a lot of fun. Adventure and exploring are in their future. As they pick up new rocks for their collections, they use identification classification, categorization, and discrimination skills.

Future careers for young rock collectors include gemologist, petroleum engineer, geologist, hydrologist, science teacher, petrographer, and petrologist.

Steig, William. *Sylvester and the Magic Pebble*. Simon & Schuster, 1969. Unpaged. Illustrated by William Steig. (P–I)

In this old and beloved story, Sylvester, the donkey, discovers a magic pebble. Upon being frightened by a lion, Sylvester wishes himself into being a rock. When he does not return home, his donkey parents, Mr. and Mrs. Duncan, begin to search frantically for Sylvester. A year passes by with no sign of Sylvester until one day Sylvester's parents go on a picnic. By great chance, they eat their meal on the very rock that is Sylvester. Mr. Duncan discovers the same pebble that Sylvester had found and places it on the rock. Sylvester wishes that he were his real self and voila! he is. A happy ending results. Steig's cartoons enhance this droll story for children.

HOBBY STARTER ACTIVITY

◼ *Crystal Growing*

Materials

> Jar for water (a clean mayonnaise jar works well)
> Liquid laundry bluing
> Salt
> Ammonia
> Box (shoebox will do)
> Rocks
> One charcoal briquette (broken into chunks)

Directions

1. In the glass jar, have the children mix ¼ cup water, ¼ cup liquid laundry bluing, and ¼ cup salt. An adult should then add 1 tablespoon of ammonia to the mixture and tell the children to avoid inhaling or swallowing the mixture and to keep it away from their eyes. This is an excellent time to draw attention to the precautionary label on the ammonia container.
2. Place rocks and charcoal pieces in box.
3. Carefully spoon the bluing mixture over the rocks and broken charcoal pieces.
4. Set aside for twenty hours.
5. Have children observe the crystal forming process. Think about and consider the following:

What does crystal growing have to do with rocks? Many substances including some types of rocks result from crystallization. Rocks that are formed from crystallization are quartz, granite, and feldspar. Other substances that form crystals are the cholesterol in our bodies, some hard candies, snowflakes, salt, sugar, mothballs, and aspirin. Knowing about the crystallization process is relevant to various fields of study. To understand crystal formation is to have the basics for understanding chemistry, geology, medicine, and pharmacology.

LANGUAGE ARTS ACTIVITY

▪ *Petroglyphs and the Sidewalk Chalk Connection*

Carved in stone is another way to talk about petroglyphs, those stone walls upon which ancient people carved symbolic or pictographic messages.

The act of leaving messages on hard surfaces may also be observed in graffiti, the Ten Commandments in the Moses story, tombstones, writing with chalk on slate, Egyptian hieroglyphics, egg painting, and even sidewalk chalk drawings. Have the children make their mark with homemade chalk. As a group, use the following recipe to make sidewalk chalk.

Materials

Masking tape

Paper tubes (such as those used for paper towels or toilet paper)

Clean plastic margarine tub

⅔ cup plaster of paris powder (be sure to read the label)

3 tablespoons tempera paint

Water

Liquid dish soap

Directions

1. Prepare the tube by cutting a section 2 inches long and taping one end shut with masking tape.
2. In the plastic container, mix the plaster of paris, the tempera paint, and a squirt of liquid soap.
3. Mix in water two tablespoons at a time until the mixture feels like thick batter.
4. Pour the batter into the cardboard tube. Let it stand for several hours.
5. Repeat the process for other colors as desired.
6. Go outside to decorate sidewalks, driveways, and playground surfaces as appropriate and permitted.

POEM

Soto, Gary. "Ode to El Moleajete." In *Neighborhood Odes*. Harcourt Brace Jovanovich, 1992.

VOCABULARY GROWTH WORDS

Atom: The smallest combining particle of an element.

Carbon: A nonmetallic element found in all organic compounds.

Cleavage: The splitting of minerals along flat surfaces.

Core: The metallic center of the Earth.

Crystal: An element of certain rocks with geometric faceted shape.

Element: A substance that cannot be broken into other substances.

Fossil: The preserved remains of plants and animals.

Igneous: A type of rock formed by intense heat.

Metamorphic: A type of rock that has been formed by the changing of another rock by heat or pressure.

Sedimentary: A type of rock formed by the deposit of sediments.

RESOURCES

Mineralogical Society of America
1015 Eighteenth Street, N.W.
Suite 601
Washington, DC 20036-5274
http://www.minsocam.org

   This society of professional mineralogists maintains a Web site that includes an "Ask a Mineralogist" page and a page titled "K–12 Education," which offers links for both students and teachers. Children will find games, and teachers will find instructional activities related to rocks, rock identification, and minerals.

READ MORE ABOUT IT

Gordon, Maria. *Rocks and Soil*. Raintree Steck-Vaughn, 1996. 32p. Illustrated by Mike Gordon. (P)

   Part of the Simple Science series, this book tells in simple text and cartoon illustrations the connection between soil and rock. Explanations tell how soil is composed of small rocks, minerals, decomposed plants and animals, and water. Mineral containing soil turns slowly into rock over a long period of time. Experiments and activities are scattered throughout the text. Readers are asked to observe various actions of soil and rocks and are told what to look for. Observation is one of the beginning steps of being a good scientist and this book reinforces that skill. For hobbyists, the book includes more than 15 projects and activities for further exploration of rocks and soil.

Meltzer, Milton. *Gold! The True Story of Why People Search for It, Mine It, Trade It, Steal It, Mint It, Hoard It, Shape It, Wear It, Fight and Kill for It.* HarperCollins, 1993. 168p. (I)

Award-winning author, Milton Meltzer explores the properties of gold and the significance that gold has had on the world's economics, history, and social structure. From ancient times to today's high-tech world, gold has been esteemed for financial value and utility to industry. Gold's value is a result of its scarcity and the cost and difficulty of mining it, as well as its usefulness and its prized beauty. The greed of mine owners has led to the present-day exploitation of child miners in Peru, the Makuna natives of Columbia, and blacks in South Africa. Millions have worked and died to make a few wealthy. Meltzer, as in his book *Potatoes*, has shown his readers the dark side of a commodity.

Pough, Frederick H. *Peterson First Guide to Rocks and Minerals.* Houghton Mifflin, 1991. 128p. (I)

Written for the serious beginning rock and mineral hobbyist, Pough's book tells the what, how, why, and where of rocks and minerals. Colored photographs make identification easy. This small-sized book can lead to a worldwide interest in rock collecting as well as careers in gemology, chemistry, geography, architecture, mathematics, and mineralogy.

Selsam, Millicent E., and Joyce Hunt. *A First Look at Rocks.* Walker, 1984. 32p. Illustrated by Harriett Springer. (P–I)

Selsam's science books survive on library shelves because of her scientific credibility and the ease with which she conveys complex scientific information to young readers. Such is the case with *A First Look at Rocks*. Along with co-author, Joyce Hunt, she explains the three main classes of rocks: igneous, sedimentary, and metamorphic. Children are told what to look for in terms they can understand. A map of the United States shows where the three main types of rocks may be found. Adults looking for an easy-to-read nonfiction book for an emergent reader and rock hound will find it here. Children looking for something to become interested in might look at other titles in this excellent series.

Stangl, Jean. *Crystals and Crystal Gardens You Can Grow.* Franklin Watts, 1990. 64p. (P–I)

To understand rocks and minerals you need to understand crystals and crystal formation. Most rocks and minerals are made up of crystals. Crystals may also be found in plant-derived substances such as sugar, which comes from sugarcane and sugar beets. Growing and studying crystals can be done with simple household objects: spoons, glasses, disposable margarine tubs, or pie pans. Nine activities are described in addition to directions for growing 10 varieties of crystal gardens. A section explaining how the gardens grew and observations that need to be made completes the book.

SCRAPBOOK CONSTRUCTION

We are living wonderful lives and we want to remember the events that mark the special days of our lives. Scrapbook construction helps us keep track of those tiny moments that accumulate to form a lifetime. It provides a way for us look back over the past months to discover patterns and to celebrate once again our first day of school, our first school dance, our best sport event, and a special birthday. Collecting, organizing, and formatting are skills used as one constructs a scrapbook.

Archivist, historian, author, journalist, photographer, and graphic artist are careers that may appeal to the person who enjoyed keeping track of life events as a child.

Provensen, Alice. *My Fellow Americans: A Family Album.* Brown Deer Press, 1995. 61p. Illustrated by Alice Provensen. (I)

In Provensen's prize-winning style, we are treated to American history in photo-album style. Famous Americans are portrayed in categories, for example, Poets in Motion, Pastoral Protectors, and Inspired Prophets. Each category features a quote from a leader in the field; dancing for example, has a definitive quote by Agnes D. Mille. This book is a fascinating way for young people to develop a concept of history and what it means to be a part of the United States family. Historical notes are provided in the back.

HOBBY STARTER ACTIVITY

▪ *Make a Memory Scrapbook*

Scrapbooks made by adults gifted with artistic eyes and manual dexterity can be intimidating to little people just starting out, so this is a K.I.S.S. (keep it simple, sweetie) type project, a concertina memory book.

First, help the children decide upon a theme for their books. Themes could be: My Baseball Hobby, My Friends, My Trip to Disney World, My Grandmother, or My Nature Hike. Guide them as they collect the memorabilia and materials for this project, for example baseball theme stickers, scorecards, and a team picture. Next, set aside time and materials to make the scrapbooks.

Materials

Paper (all types)	Pinking shears
Rolls of untreated white shelf paper	Markers
Heavy cardboard (two pieces each 9" x 12")	Ribbons
	Photographs
Stickers	Memorabilia (tickets, post cards, paper souvenirs)
Pencils	
Calligraphy markers	Envelopes
Magazines	Catalogs and magazine pictures
Regular scissors	

Directions

1. Have the children cut pieces of heavy cardboard into two 9-by-12-inch pieces.
2. Have them glue pretty paper (two pieces, 10 by 13 inches) onto the heavy cardboard by folding the paper over the cardboard pieces to make the front and back covers.
3. Have the children create a long, 8½-by-110-inch strip of paper. This is most easily accomplished by cutting untreated plain white shelf or butcher paper to the correct size.
4. Have the children accordion pleat this long strip of paper so that they have the paper folded into 10, 8½-by-11-inch segments.
5. Have them smear glue all over the back of one book cover and attach one end page of the accordion pleated strip to it. Repeat for the other cover.
6. Have them categorize, arrange, and glue their memorabilia to the pages.
7. Using decorative stickers, rubber stamps, ribbon, and paper cut with pinking scissors, have them embellish and decorate their books.

LANGUAGE ARTS ACTIVITY

▣ *Scrapbook Captions*

Photographs, memorabilia, as well as whole pages need titles and clever captions to spark up the pages and to move the text along. Tell the children to study the pictures, photographs, and themes on each page. Ask them to think what the animal or person in a photo might be thinking or saying, or what clever comment could be made about the page's contents. Have them write an appropriate caption on fancy-edged paper to glue onto the page or under the photographs.

POEM

"When on This Page You Look." In *A Rocket in My Pocket* compiled by Carl Withers. Holt, Rinehart & Winston, 1948.

VOCABULARY GROWTH WORDS

Acid free: Paper that has a pH of 7.0 or more.

Adhesive: A substance used to stick things together.

Archival: Used to describe objects, such as papers and photographs, that are treated in such a manner to last several generations.

Borders: The decorative edge surrounding a page often created by repeating a pattern.

Collage: A type of artwork in which mixed media, often various patterned paper shapes and textures, are used.

Die cut shapes: Shapes created by a device constructed for the purpose of cutting out many objects of the same shape.

End papers: The papers, often decorated, at the front and back of a book attached to the front and back covers.

Marbling: A process of placing paper atop thickened water that contains swirls of acrylic paint in order to achieve the streaked, mottled, or veined look of marble.

Memorabilia: Collections of scraps, reminders, and records of people's lives, their events, and the places where the events happened.

Polyethylene: A flexible, frosted plastic commonly used as sheet protectors.

Polypropylene: A flexible, translucent plastic.

Signature: The stack of paper that make up a book section.

RESOURCES

Jangle.com Scrapbooking and Memory Crafts
http://www.jangle.com/craft/scrapbooking/scrapbooking.htm
   This Web site is maintained by Accu-Cut, a manufacturer of cutting and die-cutting instruments for crafters. The "Tips and Techniques" section is a collection of helpful articles, including a "Mom and Me Scrap Time" page that provides ideas and guidance for including children in the scrapbook-making hobby.

Scrapbooking.com
http://www.scrapbooking.com
   This Web site provides information and tips about scrapbook creation. In addition, users will find descriptions of tools and materials for sale through the site's online store. "Beginners" is a helpful page for those who are just starting out.

READ MORE ABOUT IT

Diehn, Gwen. *Making Books that Fly, Fold, Wrap, Hide, Pop-up, Twist and Turn: Books for Kids to Make*. Lark Books, 1998. 96p. (I)
   A book that charms and informs by turn, this text on book construction will appeal to both youngsters and their adult friends. Many imaginative ideas are presented including a time capsule book, a map-folded storybook, an origami form research book, a scroll book, a pop-up book, a dos à dos book, and a lotus book form.
   In addition to easy-to-follow, step-by-step directions, Diehn includes historical tidbits about various books and libraries and full-color photos of children constructing books. This book is a gem, one sure to be treasured.

McNeill, Suzanne, and Lani Stiles, contributors. *Family Scrapbook Paper Pizzazz!* Betterway Publications, 1997. 128p. (P–A)
   This is a collection of jazzy, colorful, figured background papers that may be used to construct a scrapbook. Users are given permission to reproduce the pages for family but not commercial use. This is a great tool for ardent scrapbookers.

Packham, Jo. *Moments to Remember: The Art of Creating Scrapbook Memories*. Andrew McMeel, 1998. 128p. (I–A)
   Written for the serious adult family archivist, this book emphasizes the selection of proper archival materials, the enhancement of photographs by using computer technology, and the proper ways to photograph. Packham has an artist's eye so she stresses techniques to create gorgeous background pages for mounting photographs and family documents. A young person beginning a scrapbook would receive lots of ideas and inspiration from perusing this book's pages. Packham also includes directions for constructing various memory boxes, and she has added pages of reproducible clip art to enhance a young hobbyist's scrapbook.

Stowell, Charlotte. *Making Books*. Kingfisher, 1994. 40p. Illustrated by Jim Robins. (P–I)

Part of the Step-by-Step series, this book tells young readers how to construct a good variety of books. Pop-ups, zigzag, and hand-bound book directions are given. The author also gives directions for a wheel book. Robins's attractive, clear, and colorful illustrations make the projects easy to do. There are projects and directions that a six-year-old can follow, such as the zigzag book, as well as slightly more complicated projects such as a sewn book that a 10-year-old can do without adult help.

Vanessa-Ann. *Making Scrapbooks: Complete Guide to Preserving Your Treasured Memories*. Sterling, 1998. 128p. (I–A)

One of the great joys of making a scrapbook is the myriad tools used. Fancy edge-making scissors must be a growth industry. There was a time when the only option was a pair of Great-grandmother's pinking shears, but today there is a variety to choose from. Vanessa-Ann supplies pages and pages of tool and material descriptions with corresponding photographs. She gives specific directions for specialty scrapbooks and includes reproducible patterns and templates so that the scrapbook crafter ends up with a professional-looking product. By following the directions and suggestions given, every page in your scrapbook will be a unique, beautiful work of art. This is a book adults can use to guide children in their scrapbook construction.

22

SHOW BIZ

Let's bring back vaudeville! Show biz has something for everyone. There are all kinds of talent out there. Some people sing, some tap dance, others like to paint scenery, some know how to handle money, some are socially inclined and know how to make an audience feel at home, some can move props and scenery, while some can juggle, do magic tricks, or perform acrobatic acts. There is a bit of show person in everyone.

Children who have had fun putting on neighborhood shows in their garages have the potential to be teachers, impresarios, TV directors, public speakers, actors, nightclub performers, show dancers, birthday party performers, and singers. So when you hear a child announce, "Hey! Let's put on a play!" you will know that child is on the way to a successful life.

Ackerman, Karen. *Song and Dance Man*. Alfred A. Knopf, 1988. Unpaged. Illustrated by Stephen Gammell. (P)

Grandpa, a retired vaudeville performer, delights his young grandchildren with a soft-shoe routine, jokes and tricks that he remembers from his showman days. His grandchildren cannot be more pleased as he sings and dances his way into their memories. Gammell's lighthearted colored pencil drawings complement this upbeat story.

HOBBY STARTER ACTIVITY

▣ *Neighborhood Vaudeville and Talent Show*

Have the children organize themselves and their friends, families, and neighbors into a vaudeville show. They will need to scout out the children who can do magic tricks, perform acrobatics, juggle, dance, tell jokes, perform clown acts, sing, or play a harmonica or accordion. You will need to locate a youngster with a gift for gab to be the Master of Ceremonies to introduce the acts and to make the transitions from one act to another. A piano player to play the "traveling" music that helps to smooth out the transitions would be just the touch to make your show a success. Ask the high school music teacher for some leads.

Consider where you will have your show: church basement, community hall, senior center, someone's family room, garage, or backyard.

Consider safety issues: spotters for the acrobats, nonflammable materials, and courteous safety-minded audience members.

Consider the behind-the-scenes work: curtain pullers, publicity committee, talent scouts, director, ushers, and stagehands. You won't need scenery and the performers can provide their own props and costumes.

Consider rehearsals: performers may practice on their own. Then you will need only two to three rehearsals to work out the order and the kinks. The most important thing is to have fun safely.

LANGUAGE ARTS ACTIVITY

▣ *Show Biz Posters*

Have the children advertise their vaudeville show with posters. Urge them to make the posters big and bright and to distribute them around the neighborhood. Be sure they include time, day, date, and place. Have the children make smaller versions of the posters as fliers to distribute to people they wish to attend their vaudeville show.

POEM

Livingston, Myra Cohn. "School Play." In *Remembering and Other Poems*. McElderry, 1989.

VOCABULARY GROWTH WORDS

Character: An animal, person, or animated object in a play.

Dialogue: The lines spoken in a play.

Director: The person who organizes and coaches the actors.

Flat: An upright piece of wood painted with scenery or room interiors.

Impresario: The boss in a show business operation; the person who manages an opera or a theatrical production.

Pantomime: A play that uses gestures exclusively to communicate meaning.

Props: The objects used in a play.

Repertoire: The collection of jokes, plays, acts, patter, and songs that an actor or comedian can perform.

Skit: A short comedy act.

Vaudeville: An entertainment consisting of a series of skits, comedy acts, songs, dances, and acrobatic acts.

RESOURCES

International Jugglers Association
http://www.juggle.org
    This association is "dedicated to the advancement and promotion of juggling." They publish *Juggle* magazine and a newsletter and produce and sell videos of festivals. Since 1947, the organization has been organizing annual festivals and mini-festivals. The Web site provides information about festivals; the association's history; videos, T-shirts, and books available for purchase; and how to become a member. There is also a page of links to related Web sites. IJA has a youth membership for jugglers who are age 17 or younger.

International Brotherhood of Magicians
11155 South Towne Square, Suite C
St. Louis, MO 63123-7813
http://www.magician.org
    IBM is the world's largest organization for magicians. Through their Web site, you can obtain information about their youth program, Magical Youth, and its newsletter *Top Hat*. Magical Youth is open to kids between the ages of 12 and 18.

READ MORE ABOUT IT

Bentley, Nancy, and Donna Gutherie. *Putting on a Play: The Young Playwright's Guide to Scripting, Directing and Performing.* Millbrook Press, 1996. 64p. Illustrated by Katy Keck Arnsteen. (P–I)

Color cartoons and short chapters describe for young readers the ins and outs of play production. A committee of nine-year-olds can easily navigate this text in the morning and put on a play to entertain their parents in the evening. Points are given on how to write various kinds of plays: puppet, radio, and one-act monologues. Bentley and Gutherie tell how to rehearse and how to perform. A poem is included, as are sample scripts to help get the show into the family room. This is a highly useful book for adults and children alike.

Edin, Peter. *The Most Excellent Book of How to Be a Magician.* Copper Beech Books, 1996. 32p. Illustrated by Rob Shone. (P–I)

Nothing keeps an audience more captivated than a fast-paced magician working tricks and talking a chatty patter. Fifteen tricks are clearly and sequentially explained. Step-by-step directions show the young conjurer how to do the spectacular Tube of Mystery and the simple disappearing coin. While the tricks seem simple, they all require practice, practice, practice. Color photographs clarify the steps.

Jackman, Joan. *The Young Gymnast.* DK, 1995. 48p. Photographs by Ray Moller. (P–I)

Any good circus, vaudeville show, or talent show will need an acrobatic act. Jackman's explanations and Ray Moller's photographs show the would-be acrobat how to do cartwheels, flic flacs, headstands, and other standard acrobatic movements. Readers are shown how to link movements together in order to perform a sequence. Cautions are given about the necessity for a coach before attempting advanced moves.

Mitchelson, Mitch. *The Most Excellent Book of How to Be a Juggler.* Copper Beech Books, 1997. 32p. Illustrated by Ron Shone and Peter Harper. (P–I)

Nicely sequenced, the directions take the beginner juggler from juggling one ball to juggling nine. Variations on the juggling theme are given, as are techniques for turning a backyard pastime into a well-practiced performance. Several suggestions are given for different routines such as sharing with a buddy, the gentleperson juggler, and the bubbling juggling. The last two pages describe a clown act.

Perkins, Catherine, and Katie Roden. *The Most Excellent Book of How to Be a Clown.* Copper Beech Books, 1996. 32p. Illustrated by Rob Shone. (P–I)

The faces, costumes, and acts needed for successful clown performance are shown here. Perkins tells the young clown how to make the right moves to make a routine one that little children will love. The author emphasizes the wisdom of matching the clown's persona, costume, and accessories with the performers. Ten clown acts that can be easily practiced are carefully laid out. Directions for constructing props are given, as is a glossary.

23

STAMP COLLECTING

Stamp collecting is a popular hobby. The United States Postal Service claims that about 22 million people collect stamps. Franklin Delano Roosevelt is known to have said that if it had not been for his stamp-collecting hobby, his life would have been miserable. It is a hobby that brings happiness to solitary times yet leads to a satisfying social life as people share their collections with others. The skills that stamp collecting fosters include discrimination, categorization, knowing the art of making a deal, meticulous handling of materials, knowing the value of a stamp, research, and precision in the arrangement of stamps in an album.

Stamp collecting has the potential to lead to a lifetime interest in history, geography, philately, appraising, and trading.

Ahlberg, Janet, and Allan Ahlberg. *The Jolly Postman.* Little, Brown, 1986. Unpaged. Illustrated by Janet Ahlberg. (P)

The jolly postman delivers letters to favorite folktale characters. The actual letters are enclosed in stamped and postmarked envelopes. Pay close attention to the stamps. Their connection to the story is clever and humorous as are the other details of the letters. This whimsical book is fun for readers who are already well acquainted with the folktales.

HOBBY STARTER ACTIVITY

▪ *Begin Your Stamp Collection*

The easiest and cheapest way to start this hobby is to have the boys and girls save canceled stamps. Have them ask their grandparents, aunts, uncles, friends, and neighbors to save the envelopes that still have the canceled stamps affixed. This is a great way to strengthen intergenerational ties. Writing to grandfather to ask him to save his canceled stamps and to send them to his granddaughter just may be the start of building a more solid relationship.

LANGUAGE ARTS ACTIVITY

▪ *Listening to a Guest Speaker*

Have your group members ask around among their adult acquaintances to locate a philatelist to speak to them. Contact your town's local stamp club, which you can find by inquiring at the post office, library, or Chamber of Commerce.

Invite this expert to speak to your group for about twenty minutes; prime your group members to ask probing questions (how and why), have a 10-minute question-and-answer period, and follow this with refreshments. Remember to send thank-you notes to your speaker.

POEM

Kennedy, X. F. "Who to Trade Stamps With." In *The Kite That Braved Old Orchard Beach*. McElderry, 1991.

VOCABULARY GROWTH WORDS

Approvals: Stamps sent out by a dealer to sell to collectors.

Block: A set of four or more joined stamps.

Commemorative: Stamps that have been designed to celebrate an occasion or person.

Cover: An envelope with a canceled stamp.

Definitive: A stamp used for regular use, distinguished from a commemorative stamp.

Mint: The condition of an unused stamp.

Mint set: A collection of commemoratives issued annually by the postal service.

Philatelist: A person who collects stamps.

Plate: The printing plate.

Proof: A sheet of stamps produced by the printer to check errors before printing.

RESOURCES

American Philatelic Society
P.O. Box 8000
State College, PA 16803
http://www.stamps.org
    APS is open to both novice and experienced collectors. It offers services to its members including shows and exhibitions, accreditation of judges, and online courses to improve stamp collectors' skills. The organization also publishes a magazine and sells stamps through their Web site. The Web site includes links to "Education" and "Just for Kids" pages.

The Junior Philatelists of America
P.O. Box 2625
Albany, OR 97321
http://www.jpastamps.org
    According to their Web site, JPA is "a group run by and for young stamp collectors." Members age 17 and under are responsible for the organization's operations and the publication *The Philatelic Observer*. The Web site offers games, contests, and links to related Web sites, as well as advice about collecting.

Call 1-888-STAMP-FUN to order the United States Postal Service's Stampers Starter Kits ($9.95).

READ MORE ABOUT IT

Allen, Jody. *Usborne Guide to Stamps and Stamp Collecting.* Usborne, 1982. 32p. (I)
    Topics related to stamps and stamp collecting are treated in two-page spreads. Starting a stamp collection, handling and studying stamps, and collecting by theme are examples of the topics. Allen discusses characteristics such as mistakes, fakes, and forgeries, as well as what makes a stamp valuable. Written and published in Great Britain, this book has a global perspective.

Bolick, Nancy O'Keefe. *Mail Call! The History of the U.S. Mail Service.* Franklin Watts, 1994. 64p. (P–I)
    While most of Bolick's book is a history of the United States Postal Service; Chapter 8 is about stamps. Bolick explains the history of commemorative stamps and how a mistake can actually increase a stamp's value, for example, the Lindbergh commemorative stamp on which his airplane is depicted upside down.

Briggs, Michael. *Stamps*. Random House, 1993. 76p. (I)

One of the several books in the Hobby Handbooks series, this colorful book is sure to attract young readers to the fascinating hobby of stamp collecting. Well-diagramed and laid out, the directions for collecting and caring for stamps are easy to follow. The text is attractively arranged around colorful illustrations resulting in an accessibility that is sure to attract curious young stamp collectors. Stamp collecting inevitably leads to geography so in addition to the usual stamp-related activities, maps and foreign alphabets are included.

Granger, Neill. *Stamp Collecting*. Millbrook Press, 1994. 93p. (I)

Truly for the beginning stamp collector, this book covers the basics and beyond in an attractive manner. Plenty of white space keeps the text manageable and accessible. No topic covers more than two pages. Interwoven among the text are photographs and illustrations that give reality and visual context to the writing. Various countries and continents are covered so that the readers can connect stamp collecting with an appreciation of cultures and geography.

Hobson, Burton. *Getting Started in Stamp Collecting*. Sterling, 1982. 160p. (I)

Well beyond the needs of the beginning stamp collector, this book offers facts, figures, diagrams, black-and-white photographs, and tips for collectors 10 years old and up. American as well as worldwide stamps are described. Directions for building a collection are given, as are tips for buying and selling. The author gives the reader leads to clubs and associations. Stamp collecting may be as easy to begin as soaking off the stamp from the next letter from Grandma, but this book will point out the next step.

24 STARS

Wonder and imagination are stimulated as a child views the nighttime sky. An astronomy hobby builds skill in powers of observation, perception of pattern, mathematics, and an interest in space exploration.

Knowledge of mythology grows out of star study. Many constellations have been named for mythological characters. Greek, Roman, Native American, Asian, and African cultures have contributed to the body of stories about constellation names. Careers engendered by an early interest in astronomy include astronaut, physicist, astronomer, science teacher, folklorist, and mathematician.

Rodanas, Kristina. *Follow the Stars: A Native American Woodlands Tale*. Marshall Cavendish, 1998. Unpaged. Illustrated by Kristina Rodanas. (P–I)

Based on an Ojibwa folktale, this is the story about Wise Fisher who leads the animals to the birds of summer. Winter lasts far too long and the animals are upset. They have a meeting and Wise Fisher tells them that summer has not arrived because someone has kidnapped the birds of summer. The skeptical moose wants to know how Wise Fisher knows this. Wise Fisher replies that the stars have told him. Wise Fisher states that he will lead the animals to the birds of summer. Sure enough the animals discover that the two-legged ones have taken the birds. The animals raise such a ruckus that the two-legged ones run off. The animals feed the birds before the two-legged ones return. Return they do and they are mad! Spotting Wise Fisher, they give chase. Wise Fisher races ahead until the stars call him into the sky where he can be seen today. Rodanas's luminous illustrations create a romantic quality to the story.

HOBBY STARTER ACTIVITY

▪ *Stargazers' Club*

On a clear, moonless night gather your group together with several people from the neighborhood who have made a study of stars. Take along a star map, flashlights, and hot cocoa. Walk or drive to a spot where there is little or no artificial light: a sports field, playground, or open area in the country. It takes your eyes about 30 minutes to see clearly in the dark. After your eyes have adjusted, locate the polar constellations: the Big Dipper, the Little Dipper, and Cassiopeia.

LANGUAGE ARTS ACTIVITY

▪ *Plays Starring Stars*

Find an anthology of mythology related to stars and constellations, for example, the story of the constellation Cassiopeia. Read aloud a few myths to your group. Help them create a script based upon the myth and in reader's theater style present the play to another group. White bed sheets make great togas for the Roman myths. Don't forget to pin the backsides together when costuming the characters. Otherwise the audience will be gratuitously amused.

POEM

Bruchac, Joseph, compiler. "The Scattered Stars," a Cochiti Pueblo poem. In *The Earth Under Sky Bear's Feet: Native American Poems of the Land*. Philomel, 1995. Illustrated by Thomas Locker.

VOCABULARY GROWTH WORDS

Apogee: The most distant point from Earth that the moon reaches as it orbits the Earth.

Astronomer: A scientist who studies the origin, size, motion, and formations of stars and planets.

Circumpolar stars: Stars that never set in the northern hemisphere.

Constellation: The imaginary configurations of stars into human and animal figures.

Eclipse: The blocking from view of one celestial body by another.

Galaxy: A large system of stars, planets, and gases.

Planet: A celestial body that revolves around a star.

Revolution: The movement of a celestial body in an orbit.

Rotation: The turning around and around on an axis.

Star: A hot, luminous ball of gas seen as a point of light in the sky.

RESOURCES

American Association of Amateur Astronomers
3131 Custer Road, Suite 175
Plano, TX 75075
http://www.corvus.com/aaaa.htm

The goal of AAAA is to foster an interest in amateur astronomy by developing and promoting programs. The Web site includes links to astronomy-related sites; background information about the constellations; and First Light, an introductory astronomy kit for sale through their online store, AstroMax.

READ MORE ABOUT IT

Asimov, Isaac. *The Space Spotter's Guide.* Gareth Stevens, 1989. 32p. (P–I)

In this book, Asimov points out where to locate the major constellations of the spring, summer, autumn, and winter skies. Where, what, and how to locate the planets are also covered. This is a short guide that the young reader will value.

Ford, Harry. *The Young Astronomer.* Dorling Kindersley, 1998. 37p. (I)

Two well-laid-out pages per topic make a complex topic easy to understand. Harry Ford is the planetarium lecturer at the Old Observatory in Greenwich, England. He has translated his considerable wisdom about astronomy into an easily understood text for young hobbyists. He explains the solar system, planets, the sun, the moon, and the northern and southern hemispheres. The easy-to-do projects that are scattered throughout the book make this book perfect for children.

Hathaway, Nancy. *The Friendly Guide to the Universe: A Down-to-Earth Tour of Space, Time and the Wonders of the Cosmos.* Viking, 1994. 462p. (I)

A big fat tome, this book at first looks overwhelming but it is so well organized that a fast skim and scan will get readers to the part they might need for a report or interest. No topic is addressed in an attenuated fashion that might be discouraging. The book can be read in bits and pieces. This is a great stuck-in-traffic book for children and adults. Hathaway has a reader-friendly writing style that enlivens facts and details. Heartening mini-biographies of astronomers including Subrahmanyan Chandraskhar, known for his work on white dwarfs, Annie Jump Cannon, classifier of stars, and Henrietta Swan Leavitt, calculator of star distances are scattered throughout. Charts and sidebars give tidbits of information making this a truly friendly and humorous, yet serious guide to the universe.

Mitton, Jacqueline. *Zoo in the Sky: A Book of Animal Constellations*. National Geographic Society, 1998. 32p. Illustrated by Christina Balit. (P–I)

    The brilliance of Christina Balit's stylized illustrations sparks the reader's imagination. Paging through this book in the daytime makes readers long for a clear nighttime sky so that they can get out to see the animal constellations. Both the northern and southern skies are illustrated. Leo the lion, Draco the dragon, and the Great Bear are featured along with Lupus and Lepus and Cetus.

Sipiera, Diane M., and Paul P. Sipiera. *Constellations*. Children's Press, 1997. 48p. (P)

    Constellations is well formatted and makes complex concepts accessible to very young astronomers. Background information that tells why and how people locate constellations is given, as well as information about a few major constellations. Color photographs, sky charts, and archival photographs enhance the text. The back pages list organizations and Web sites that provide further information. This book is part of the True Book series, which includes *The Stars*, *The Solar System*, and *Galaxies*.

25

STARTING A BUSINESS

Knowledge of finance, marketing, advertising, entrepreneurship, and venture capital is derived from starting a business as a child.

Persuasive talking and writing, risk taking, handling and accounting for money, record keeping, group consensus building, leading and communicating, mathematics, problem solving, ingenuity, planning, and instructing are skills generated by starting a business.

The child who starts a business may grow up to be a banker, stockbroker, small business owner, industrial giant, public relations officer, real estate agent, purchasing agent, or salesperson.

Brown, Marc. *Arthur's Pet Business*. Little, Brown, 1990. Unpaged. Illustrated by Marc Brown. (P)

Arthur wants a puppy but his parents want him to demonstrate that he is responsible before they give their permission. Arthur decides that getting a job will do the trick but he does not like any that are available. So he goes into the pet sitting business. His first client is Perky, an ill-tempered, persnickety dog. Other pets, including a boa constrictor, soon follow. Unfortunately when Perky's owner returns, Perky is nowhere to be found. Soon she is found under Arthur's bed where she has had a litter of puppies. Mrs. Hood, Perky's owner, offers Arthur a puppy and all ends well.

25—STARTING A BUSINESS

HOBBY STARTER ACTIVITY

▣ *Taffy Pull*

Nothing sells as well as candy, and no candy-making endeavor induces the teamwork so necessary for entrepreneurship as a good old-fashioned taffy pull. However, don't go too far with this project without checking local regulations and restrictions if you plan to take it beyond the confines of family.

Before beginning the activity, instruct your group on the importance of cleanliness and safety. Cooked hot taffy syrup can cause a nasty burn so be careful. Insist on washed hands and hair pinned back, as well as calm, controlled behavior.

Materials

A heavy-bottomed pan	Kitchen scissors
Candy thermometer	Molasses
Stove	Sugar
Set of measuring cups and spoons	Water
Wooden spoons	Vinegar
Hot pads	Cream of tartar
Buttered tempered glass pan	Butter
Spatulas	Baking soda
Wax paper	

Directions

1. In the heavy-bottomed pan, have the children place:
    - ½ cup molasses
    - 1½ cups sugar
    - ½ cup water
    - 1½ tablespoons vinegar
2. Cook over medium-high heat while the children take turns stirring with a wooden spoon.
3. When the mixture comes to a boil, add ¼ teaspoon cream of tartar.
4. Have one child keep an eye on the candy thermometer. When the temperature reaches 256 degrees, stir in ¼ cup butter and ⅛ teaspoon baking soda.
5. Have an adult carefully remove the pan from the heat and pour the mixture into the buttered tempered glass pan.
6. As the candy cools, have the children fold the outside edges toward the middle with spatulas.
7. When the mixture is cool enough to handle, divide it into sections.
8. Have the children wash and butter their hands.

9. Give sections of the candy to pairs of children, and tell them to pull the taffy, fold it in half, and pull again. Have them repeat this pulling and folding process until the taffy is porous and light-colored.
10. Have them pull the taffy into a long rope and snip it into pieces.
11. Have the pieces wrapped in wax paper squares that another team has prepared.

Now you have an inventory. Count the number of pieces. Discuss how to set the price of each piece. Send the "sales team" out among family and friends to sell the taffy. Discuss the results.

LANGUAGE ARTS ACTIVITY

▪ *Creating a Business Plan*

At first, starting a business and making money is an exciting prospect for children. To help ensure that their business succeeds, help the children develop business plans. A suggested list of questions follows.

What kind of business do I/we want—service, creative, entertainment, manufacturing?

What are my/our skills?

___ good with animals

___ good with younger children

___ good at talking with adults

___ good at working with my hands

___ good at art projects and design

___ good at entertaining

___ good at organizing

___ good with numbers

___ good at working on the computer

___ good at sewing

___ good at cooking

___ good at constructing stuff

___ good at gardening, growing plants

___ good with playing games

___ good at music, singing, and playing an instrument

To whom do I/we sell? And how do I/we reach them?

What does this area need? _____

How many potential customers are there? _____

What do they read, listen to, and watch? _____

Where do potential customers live, walk, and work? _____

How do I/we figure what price to charge? _____

What laws must I/we be aware of? _____

What are my goals?

I plan to _____ (do what).

I plan to make _____ dollars.

I plan to sell _____ (how many).

I plan to provide _____ (how many).

I plan to start with _____ dollars.

I plan to run my business for _____ days (or for _____ hours).

I plan to check up on my goals on _____ (date).

I will call my business _____.

What have I/we missed? _____

Who can I/we ask about starting and running a business? _____

_____

What books can I/we read? _____

POEM

Livingston, Myra Cohn. "Lemonade Stand." In *Worlds I Know and Other Poems*. Atheneum, 1985.

VOCABULARY GROWTH WORDS

Accounting: The organizing of a business's financial record.

Balance sheet: A record of the value what the business owns (assets) and the value of what the business owes (liabilities). Subtract the liabilities from the assets and hope the results are positive.

Business plan: A written description of the product or service, how much it will cost to produce, the price of the product or service, and the anticipated profit.

Economics: The study of the flow of money and the production and distribution of goods and services.

Entrepreneur: The person who starts a business.

Inventory: The number of items on hand to be sold.

Marketing: Getting the product or service into the hands of the prospects through advertising and promotion.

Profit and loss statement: A summary of the income and expenses of a business.

Wholesale: Buying and selling goods and services among businesses.

RESOURCES

Junior Achievement International
2780 Janitell Road
Colorado Springs, CO 80906
http://www.jaintl.org

This nonprofit organization and its 158 local chapters promote free enterprise and market-driven economies. According to the Web site, JAI works to "recognize and serve Member Nations that develop and implement economic education programs for young people through a partnership between business and education." The Web site also offers information about specific programs and links to Member Nation Web pages. The site specifically for the United States branch can be accessed through the "JAI Links" page.

READ MORE ABOUT IT

Erlbach, Arlene. *The Kids' Business Book.* Lerner, 1998. 64p. (I)
    Twelve young entrepreneurs and their businesses are described. Readers learn about Scott and his lemonade stand, Jason's birthday party store, and David's better letters, to name a few. The chapter "Starting a Business" describes how to decide what business to start, how to figure out if a profit will be made, and how to advertise. This helpful guide is likely to lead children into their own successful businesses.

Halperin, Wendy Anderson. *Once Upon a Company: A True Story.* Orchard Books, 1998. 40p. (P–I)
    A story book? A business book? An inspirational book? All three and more. Joel, the young narrator, recounts how he and his sisters start a Christmas wreath company (they have supportive parents, grandparents, and neighbors) and over a period of six years they make $16 thousand. They call their company the College Fund Wreath Company. In the process of enlarging their company to salespeople, distributors, and employees, they learn the meaning of profit, promotion, wholesale, retail, and zero coupon bonds. With this book in hand, children may expand their vocabulary and wealth.

Otfinoski, Steve. *The Kid's Guide to Money.* Scholastic, 1996. 128p. (I)
    A lot of information about earning, saving, and growing money is given in this book. It is jam-packed with strategies described without too many complicating details. The author tells how to start up a business and gives plenty of helpful hints to make the business a success. The optimistic author assumes that the reader will make money and provides information about savings accounts, bonds, and stocks. He has a section on budgeting, as well as a chapter on sharing through donations of time and money. Of particular value for readers with a hobby is the section titled "Turning a Hobby into an Investment," which deals primarily with collectibles, volunteering, and borrowing.

Roper, Ingrid. *Moneymakers: Good Cents for Girls.* Pleasant Company, 1998. 110p. Illustrated by Susan Synarski. (P–I)
    Roper gives 10 essential steps that will likely lead to business success. Roper relates the true stories of seven female entrepreneurs. Seven types of businesses, such as computer-related, pet-related, and craft-related are described along with tips for starting each business. A neat addition comes at the book's end; there are ready-made price tags, bills, receipts, business cards, and doorknob flyers. Mix this book with imagination and ingenuity and expect the best.

Thompson, Terri. *Biz Kids' Guide to Success: Money-Making Ideas for Young Entrepreneurs*. Barron's, 1992. 92p. Illustrated by Shannon Keegan. (I)

One would think that every book for children that talks about making money would have a well-thought-out business plan. They don't, and that makes this book special. Not only does it provide a step-by-step map of planning out a business before starting out, it also provides the forms and worksheets to help children think it through. Well organized and easy to follow, this book helps the reader to get through the decision-making maze and to see that a successful business is a possibility. Stories of young entrepreneurs from 10 to 17 are scattered throughout, offering role models and encouragement.

26

STORYTELLING

Enormous satisfaction awaits children who become beguiled by storytelling's magic. Story selection for a storytelling program leads children to read widely and become well acquainted with many stories, especially folktales. Learning the story improves memory. Telling the story to an appreciative audience increases social and oral communication skills. Because storytelling exists in every culture, children will come to know the world's diversity through storytelling; there is not just one way to tell a story.

Youth group leader, teacher, actor, professional storyteller, children's librarian, folklorist, birthday party entertainer, and public speaker are some of the careers in the future for storytellers.

As with all hobbies, storytelling holds great potential for community service. Once a life is enriched with a passionate interest, there is much to share.

Lewin, Ted. *The Storytellers*. Morrow, 1998. Unpaged. Illustrated by Ted Lewin. (P–I)

Ted Lewin takes us on a walk through the ancient city of Fez in Morocco. As we turn the pages of this beautifully illustrated book, we pass through the wool dyer's stalls, the copper and brass souk (market), and the date souk where the sunshine filters through reed roofs. We follow the course of Abdul and his grandfather, the storyteller. They spread their blanket and release the white pigeon that flies into the air to bring back a story. The crowd gathers to listen as Grandfather tells an ancient story. Lewin's illustrations, so realistic and luminous, make it easy to imagine we are actually among the sights, sounds, and smells of Fez.

HOBBY STARTER ACTIVITY

▪ *Have Mini Flannel Board, Will Travel*

Materials

Foam board (12"-x-18" piece for each child)
Envelope (9" x 10")
Flannel (14"-x-20" piece)
Crayons
Glue
Tagboard
Flannel board miniature figures (such as a castle, cottage, fairy godmother, king, young girl heroine, young boy hero, sinister adult female, sinister adult male)

Directions

1. Help the children cover the foam board or suitable substitute (a used lap writing board or heavy cardboard) by gluing the flannel to the board.
2. Glue the envelope to the back so that the figures may be stored there.
3. Duplicate the figures on the following pages (Figures 26.1, 26.2, 26.3, 26.4). Help the children cut them out and glue them to tagboard. Create additional characteristics as needed.
4. Have the children color in the details. Help them cut flannel strips and glue these strips to backs of each of the figures.
5. Encourage your group members to make up their own stories using the figures.
6. Have them search for props in magazines and catalogs or have the children draw them. Props could be campfires, a pig, a black pot, and a fancy bottle, or anything that would add details to their own stories.

Hobby Starter Activity ■ 129

Figure 26.1. Adult man.

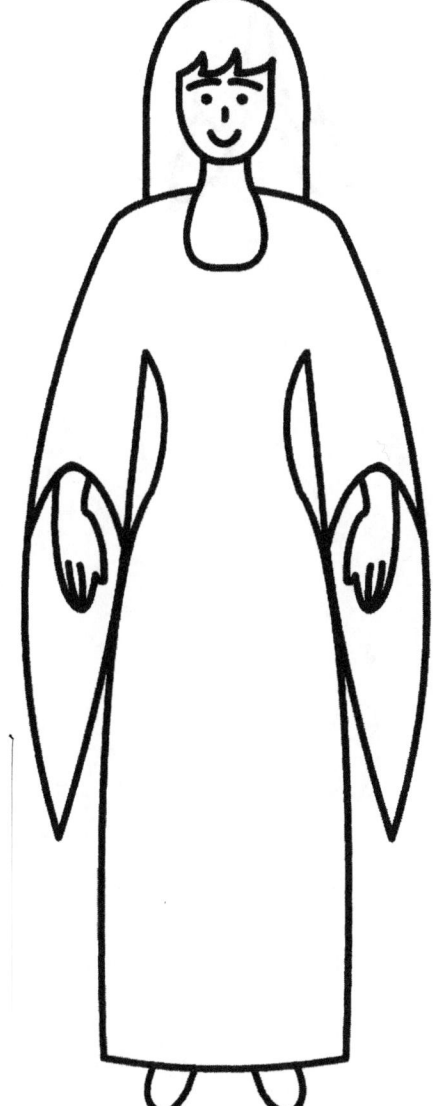

Figure 26.2. Adult woman.

130 ■ 26—STORYTELLING

Figure 26.3. Young boy.

Figure 26.4. Young girl.

LANGUAGE ARTS ACTIVITY

▪ *Audience Participation Story*

Pickin' Peas by Margaret Read MacDonald has the makings for a fun audience participation story. This is a story about a young gardener and a pesky, mischievous rabbit. Have your students learn the story. Here are some suggested steps:

1. Read or tell the story to the children. Tape recording the reading helps.
2. On chart paper or chalkboard, block the main events of the story with your group.
3. Have the children accordion pleat a long strip of adding machine tape (approximately 48 inches long). On each frame, have them draw an event from the story in order. Stick figures are good for this. They may wish to write down the repeated lines where they appear in the story.
4. Have them decide which parts of the story are appropriate for audience participation—the repeated lines of the rabbit and those of the gardener.
5. Have the children memorize the story. Reassure them that they do not need to learn the story by heart. It is best told in their own words.
6. Find groups of younger children for your group to tell the story to.
7. Personally give each storyteller an enormous amount of praise.

POEM

Silverstein, Shel. "Invitation." In *Where the Sidewalk Ends*. HarperCollins, 1974.

VOCABULARY GROWTH WORDS

Character: A person, animal, or animated object that plays a role in a story.

Emphasis: The stress given to a word or words by saying the word or words a little louder.

Expression: The ability of storytellers to put appropriate feeling in their voices to match the feeling of the story characters or action.

Eye contact: The ability to look at the faces in all sections of the audience.

Folktale: An animal story from the oral tradition of common people handed down from one generation to the other.

Gestures: The movement of hands and arms to convey story action or feeling.

Memorization: The process of learning a story or poem by heart.

Self-esteem: The feelings of pride engendered in a person by praise from self and others.

Stage fright: The attack of nerves that hits performers before they begin to perform.

Visualization: The ability to see story, setting, character, and action in the mind's eye or imagination.

RESOURCES

Storytelling Foundation International
116 West Main Street
Jonesborough, TN 37659
http://www.storytellingfoundation.com/home.htm

    This nonprofit organization promotes the art of storytelling through educational programs. Located in the small town of Jonesborough, Tennessee, the organization produces the National Storytelling Festival held every October. The Web site states, "Storytelling Foundation International is initially focusing on the creative applications of storytelling in the areas of health and healing; conflict prevention and resolution; leadership and management; and children, youth, and families."

READ MORE ABOUT IT

Bruchac, Joseph. *Tell Me a Tale: A Book About Storytelling*. Harcourt Brace, 1997. 144p. (I)

    Based upon a model of observing, listening, remembering, and sharing, Bruchac constructs this treatise for telling stories. Stories, he believes, teach us lessons about how to live our lives. Stories give us insight into why people do the things they do and the consequences of those actions. He wants boys and girls to understand that stories and storytelling deepen a child's vision and spiritual wisdom. Poignant examples of this are Bruchac's stories that transform anger and heal pain. The reader is left hoping that there will be hundreds of Bruchacs going to high schools to help heal wounded young people with stories. Maybe when enough young people have taken Bruchac's wisdom to their hearts by listening, observing, and remembering, they will share the healing power of storytelling.

Griffin, Barbara Budge. *Storyteller's Handbook: A Guidebook for Story Research and Learning*. Griffin McKay, 1990. 120p. (I)

    A good, basic guide, Griffin's book contains particularly valuable tools for learning a story. She includes devices such as story maps, story setting worksheets, character study forms, and story clustering worksheets. She provides helpful hints for warming-up exercises such as tongue twisters. Comprehensive, specialized bibliographies aid the story seeker and collector. A glossary is included.

Hamilton, Martha, and Mitch Weiss. *Stories in My Pocket: Tales Kids Can Tell*. Fulcrum, 1997. 192p. Illustrated by Annie Campbell. (I)

Written for kids who want to tell stories, the neat aspects of this book are the side-by-side columns. The left column is the story as it needs to be told. The right column tells the teller the gestures and tone of voice to use. Thirty stories and the directions to follow are divided into four levels from Starter Stories to Most Challenging Stories. In this manner the beginning storyteller is eased along the path to competency. The last section tells adults how they can support the fledgling entertainer.

MacDonald, Margaret Read. *Pickin' Peas*. HarperCollins, 1998. 32p. Illustrated by Pat Cummings. (P)

A perfect read-aloud story, *Pickin' Peas* lends itself to audience participation, pantomime and storytelling. A little girl catches the rabbit that was eating her peas. He tricks her into letting him out of his box so he can dance for her. Closer and closer the crafty rabbit gets to an open window and finally freedom. MacDonald has provided the musical score to the chant that is repeated throughout the story. This story calls out to teachers and youth group leaders to be used and loved.

Tashjian, Virginia. *Juba This and Juba That*. Little, Brown, 1995. 106p. Illustrated by Nadine Bernard Westcott. (I)

For the young, experienced storytellers, this compilation is sure to add zest to their storytelling programs. In addition to the eight lively audience participation stories, Tashjian includes chants, limericks, rhymes, riddles, songs, and tongue twisters that will spice up the storytelling hour. Most invite the audience to participate and to get up out of their seats to move as the chant or song suggests.

27
TEDDY BEARS

Symbols of comfort and affection, teddy bears, a perennial favorite, bring a smile and reassurance to those who receive them. They have become our society's furry messengers of love. Teddy bears convey the thoughts, "I'm thinking of you. Somebody cares about you." Often policemen, firemen, nurses, and paramedics supply themselves with teddy bears to use in cases of emergencies when children are involved.

People enjoy collecting teddy bears because of their appealing attributes. Some are pretty; some are whimsical; some are valuable as antiques. Learning to make a teddy bear involves perceptual motor skills, eye-hand coordination, spatial relationship skills, and fine muscle coordination.

A keen passion for teddy bears could lead to a career in the toy industry, folk art, design, appraising, and toy repair and refurbishment.

Alborough, Jez. *It's the Bear*. Candlewick Press, 1994. Unpaged. Illustrated by Jez Alborough. (P)

Described by the author/illustrator as a slapstick comedy for children, the book lives up to its billing through the exaggerated size of the bear and his teddy bear. In this sequel to *Where's My Teddy?* Eddie and his fearless mom go for a picnic in the woods. Eddie fears that the bear will be there despite his mom's reassurances, but when she goes back to the house to fetch the pie, along comes the feared great big bear that is delighted to find a picnic basket. When the bear opens the picnic basket, he gets a surprise.

HOBBY STARTER ACTIVITY

▪ *Terry Cloth Teddy Bear*

Materials

Old terry cloth towels, washcloths (You will need a minimum of two 6½"-x-7½" pieces for each bear.)
Thread
Needles with large eyes
Pattern (provided below)
Soap chips (have your group's families contribute soap fragments)
Buttons
Embroidery thread, black or brown

Directions

1. Using the bear pattern (Figure 27.1), cut out two pieces of terry cloth.
2. On one piece, sew button eyes and embroider a mouth and nose with black or brown embroidery floss.
3. Sew the two pieces together using a blanket stitch, leaving open a 2-inch space.
4. Stuff bear with soap chips.
5. Complete the sewing.

Note: If the washcloth bear is to be a gift to a baby, do not sew on button eyes. They could come off and endanger the baby. Instead, use embroidery for the eyes. If the bear is to be a gift to a child or baby, use only mild soap for the chips. If the bear is to be a gift for use in the kitchen, use kitchen soap, such as Fels Naptha.

Hobby Starter Activity ■ 137

Figure 27.1. Teddy bear pattern.

LANGUAGE ARTS ACTIVITY

◼ *Teddy Bear Celebration*

People celebrate Teddy Roosevelt's birthday and Teddy Bear Day on October 27. A week or so before the special day, send out teddy bear-shaped invitations to a teddy bear celebration to all the neighborhood families. Invite the children, mothers, fathers, grandparents, aunts, uncles, and cousins to bring their teddy bears. Be sure your children know what to put on an invitation (what, when, and where), and the importance of the please respond request. Decorate the envelopes with teddy bear stamps. *Note:* Some people celebrate Teddy Bear Day on July 10.

Suggested Entertainment

Sing several verses of the "Teddy Bear's Picnic."

Tell teddy bear jokes.

Read aloud a teddy bear picture book.

Go on a "bear hunt." (Michael Rosen has retold the story in a book illustrated by Helen Oxenbury titled *We're Going on a Bear Hunt.* This is a classic participation story for children.)

Play an adaptation of "Farmer in the Dell" and call it "Teddy Bear in His Den."

Jump rope and chant the "Teddy Bear, Teddy Bear Turn Around" jump rope rhyme.

Refreshments

Gingerbread cookies

Cinnamon toast using bear-shaped bread

Punch

POEM

Chute, Marchette. "My Teddy Bear." In *Read-Aloud Rhymes for the Very Young* selected by Jack Prelutsky. Alfred A. Knopf, 1986.

Hillert, Margaret. "My Teddy Bear." In *Read-Aloud Rhymes for the Very Young* selected by Jack Prelutsky. Alfred A. Knopf, 1986.

VOCABULARY GROWTH WORDS

Arctophiles: People who are enthusiastic about bears.

Kapok: Fiber from the seeds of the tropical tree *Ceiba pentandra* used to stuff toy bears.

Mohair: Cloth woven from Angora goat fleece.

October 27: Teddy Bear Day. The birthday of Theodore Roosevelt when teddy bear enthusiasts hold picnics and celebrations.

Plush: Soft, fuzzy fabric used for making teddy bears.

Winnie the Pooh: Toy bear made famous by the author A. A. Milne.

RESOURCES

Good Bears of the World
P.O. Box 13097
Toledo, OH 43613
(419) 531-5365
http://www.goodbearsoftheworld.org
   Members of this organization donate teddy bears worldwide to children in need.

READ MORE ABOUT IT

Bjork, Christina. *Big Bear's Book*. Raben and Sjogren, 1994. 76p. (I)
   This fanciful autobiography of Big Bear mixes historical fact and teddy bear fiction. Big Bear tells of his life with the other toys and human friends living in Christina's home. Family anecdotes and photographs lend creditability. Historical, psychological, and economic facts are scattered throughout the book. The last section contains listings of teddy bear literature, museums, and the address of the Good Bears of the World.

Erlbach, Arlene. *Teddy Bears*. Carolrhoda Books, 1997. 48p. (P–I)
   What a delightful look at history with a teddy bear theme! How and why we got from hard wooden toys to mass-produced soft stuffed ones turns out to be a function of social economic trends as well as happenstance. Erlbach explains how the movement of children from farms to cities between the 1860s and the early 1900s caused a demand for more toys and that by 1906, American toy factories in every major American city were meeting the demand. About 250 million dollars are spent on teddy bears nowadays. Erlbach retells the Teddy Roosevelt story and his connection with Rose and Morris Michton, the creators of the teddy bear. A glossary and directions for a Teddy Bear Picnic are included.

Garcia, Jerry, and David Grisman. *The Teddy Bear's Picnic*. HarperCollins, 1996. Illustrated by Bruce Whately. (P–I)

    Bruce Whately's illustrations done in warm, soft tones make this book appropriate for the preschool set for which it is intended. A tape of the beloved song is included with the book. The lyrics of the song comprise the story line of the book.

Marzollo, Jean. *The Teddy Bear Book*. Dial Books for Young Readers, 1989. Unpaged. Illustrated by Ann Schweninger. (P)

    Adapted jump rope rhymes, ball-bouncing chants, and more are collected here for your enjoyment. This is a perfect complement to teddy bear collecting, construction, and picnics. Your teddy bear celebrations will be enlivened. Hopefully there is a soccer team called Teddy Bears somewhere in this land that could be cheered on to victory with the strawberry shortcake cheer. Ann Schweninger's droll pictures add to the book's cute appeal.

Morris, Ann. *How Teddy Bears Are Made: A Visit to the Vermont Teddy Bear Factory*. Scholastic, 1994. Unpaged. Photographs by Ken Heyman. (P)

    This is a simple photo essay about the tour taken by three preschool children in a teddy bear factory. The sequence of assembly line bear manufacturing from concept to stamping out the parts to dressing to shipping is laid out.

28

TOYS

Tops, yo-yos, jacks-in-a-box, marbles, bouncing balls, and gliding paper airplanes are all delightful items that fill an active child's playtime and incite activity, playfulness, manipulation, surprise, spontaneity, and social interaction. Whether played with, constructed, or collected, toys are valued by children in every culture. Children everywhere take delight in the whirring, clicking, spinning, and swinging of toys.

Toy lovers grow up to be toy department managers, toy buyers, toy creators, toy collectors, CEOs, and even presidents of the United States.

Dugan, Barbara. *Loop the Loop*. Greenwillow, 1992. Unpaged. Illustrated by James Stevenson. (P–I)

Stevenson's droll cartoons match Dugan's snappy, heartwarming story. A little girl, Anne, makes good friends with Mrs. Simpson, a colorful senior citizen in a wheelchair who is highly adept with the yo-yo and witty comebacks. Mrs. Simpson thinks it's high time for Anne to learn the fine points of yo-yo tricks. She demonstrates Walk the Dog, Around the World, and Loop the Loop. Her demonstration captivates Anne who immediately borrows a book on yo-yo tricks from the local library and begins practicing. Unfortunately, one day Mrs. Simpson breaks her hip and becomes greatly disheartened. When Anne visits Mrs. Simpson in the nursing home, she sneaks in Mrs. Simpson's cat, Bertrand, for a visit and puts on a snappy performance with her yo-yo tricks. Mrs. Simpson is cheered by Anne's visit. Mrs. Simpson is one lucky lady surrounded by gentle people who treat her with compassion.

HOBBY STARTER ACTIVITY

■ *Make a Toy Contest*

Materials

Brads	Tape
Rubber bands	Egg cartons
Cardboard scraps	Margarine tubs
Tagboard	Match boxes
Empty spools	Pencil compass
Dowels	Pencils
Nuts	Paper
Bolts	Batteries
Screws	Copper wire
Springs	Balsa wood
Glue	Modeling clay
Stapler	

Directions

Using these materials, your creativity, and your imagination, create a toy. We will have a contest to decide who has created a toy that might fall into one of these categories:

- Funniest
- Most useful
- Prettiest
- Best application of mathematics
- Works best
- Moves farthest
- Moves fastest
- Most clever
- Goes the highest
- Noisiest
- Most original
- Cutest

Note: You want to have as many categories (or more) as children. Be certain everyone gets a prize.

LANGUAGE ARTS ACTIVITY

■ *Children Have Always Wanted to Have Fun: A Research Project*

Have your group research the history of toys. Use the following resources and ways to gather information:

1. Interview families in the neighborhood to discover who has toys and stories and marvelous old toys.
2. Search the Internet to find toy museum sites. Try http://www.ala.org/parentspage/greatsites/amazing.html.
3. Research old catalogs, such as Sears Roebuck, to find pictures and descriptions.
4. Invite curators of your town's museum to give a program on old children's toys in the museum's collection.

As the culmination project, have your group create a museum of toys from the past by collecting toys from families in their neighborhood. Seek out and include as many cultures as possible, such as apple granny dolls from Appalachia, worry dolls from Guatemala, and bobbing head toys from India.

Have the children write reports on some aspect of toys and give an oral presentation to another group of children, preferably in your group's toy museum setting.

POEM

Paxton, Tom. *The Marvelous Toy*. Morrow Junior Books, 1996.

VOCABULARY GROWTH WORDS

Bobbing head toy: A toy made on the principle of discovering the object's balancing point.

Glider: An airfoil that moves through the air empowered by a push.

Pull toys: Wooden wheeled toys with a cord attached for pulling. Antique ones are valuable.

Soft toy: A toy, usually stuffed, made for cuddling and hugging. It is often in the form of an animal.

Top: A rounded toy, wider at the top and pointed at the bottom, operated by winding string around the bottom section and then with a jerk of the string, setting the top free to spin.

Wind-up toy: Mechanical toy that operates by winding a spring with a key and then releasing the toy.

RESOURCES

International Top Spinners Association
612 Southwest Summit
Lawton, OK 73501
http://byron.com/itsa

    The International Top Spinners Association is "an organization that specializes in the hobby and sport of spinning tops." The Web site offers related links and books, membership information, and a page of tricks.

READ MORE ABOUT IT

Caney, Steven. *Steven Caney's Toy Book*. Workman, 1972. 176p. (P–I)
    First published in 1972 and now reissued, this book is full of inventive ideas for child-constructed toys. Imaginations are sure to be sparked by these ideas. This is a book that has deservedly won the praise of museums and book reviewers. An observant child will discover scientific principles while having fun making tire swings, parachutes, racing spools, and propeller sticks. Fifty-one ideas are collected here.

Doney, Meryl. *Toys*. Franklin Watts, 1995. 32p. (P–I).
    A trip around the world via toys is mapped out for readers by Doney. She describes how to make toys that are representative of India, Guatamala, Russia, Japan, Africa, Poland, Sweden, and the United States. The straightforward directions are easily followed whether we are learning how to construct a truck, fashioning worry dolls, or making a mini kite. Some steps require adult assistance; these are marked with a symbol. A list of toy museums to visit is provided, as is a glossary.

Hauser, Jill Frankel. *Gizmos and Gadgets: Creating Science Contraptions That Work (and Knowing Why)*. Williamson, 1999. 144p. Illustrated by Michael Kline. (P–I)
    Experienced teacher Jill Hauser explains how to create more than 75 whatchamacallits that will captivate a child's playful imagination. Science is thrown in for good measure but with these fun-filled activities no one will have to tell children, "Do this because it is good for you." This is another winner from Williamson Publishing.

Wallace, Mary. *I Can Make Toys*. Greey de Pencier Books, 1994. 32p. Photographs by Mary Wallace. (P)
    A beginning reader and an avid toy maker will be able to enjoy this book and make the toys described. Mary Wallace's colorful photographs that show each step guarantee success. Toy makers will be able to make wheeled tops that really move, a stuffed bunny from a sock, a toy doll house from a shoe box and tiny people from

twist-ties. Summer afternoons or rainy days will be more enjoyable with this book, its materials, imaginative children and, an interested grown-up.

Zubrowski, Bernie. *Tops: Building and Experimenting with Spinning Toys*. Morrow Junior Books, 1989. 96p. Illustrated by Roy Doty. (P–I)

A Boston Children's Museum Activity Book, this book reveals to intermediate grade readers how to make a variety of yo-yos and spinning tops. Illustrated by Roy Doty's cartoons, the book is sure to attract young toy makers. However, no matter how simple the toy creation, children need adult help to get through the step-by-step sequences. Each toy explanation includes a "What's Happening" section to help youngsters develop a scientific way of observation.

29

TRAINS

The sight and sound of a model railroad train circling the Christmas village under the tree is a cherished memory for many.

There is something mysteriously alluring about this hobby that is passed from one generation to another. For some it is the power to create a world of one's own making. For others it is the fascination with electronics and the control over the switches. Still for others it is a fascination with the trains themselves.

For adults it is often a hobby of recovery. After having settled into home, career, and family, many people cast about searching for something else to occupy them, and they remember their childhood model train hobby. They return to it with remarkable avidity. Electronic, civil and mechanical engineering, urban planning, landscape architecture, mathematics, and the railroad industry are careers that may result from an early interest in model trains.

Brown, Margaret Wise. *The Train to Timbuctoo*. Golden Books, 1999. Unpaged. Illustrated by Art Seiden. (P)

Of course the book title rhymes with Kalamazoo! This 1999 reprint of Brown's 1951 classic features Art Seiden's original artwork. Rhyme, repetition, and contrast characterize the text that tells the story of a big train and a fanciful little train as they chug from Kalamazoo to Timbuctoo.

HOBBY STARTER ACTIVITY

▪ *Oatmeal Container Tunnel and Mountain*

The cylindrical cartons in which oatmeal is sold make ideal tunnels for a model railroad layout. Have your group members assemble the following materials.

Materials

Cylindrical oatmeal containers
Tagboard
Masking tape
Newspapers
Wheat paste (1 package)
Plastic pails
White glue
Paper towels
Tempera paints (green, brown, gray)
Paintbrushes

Directions

1. Attach the oatmeal container to the tagboard with masking tape.
2. Shred some of the newspaper.
3. Crumple other newspaper pages into odd shapes, some rounded, some elongated.
4. Glue and tape the crumpled newspaper pieces onto the oatmeal container to create the shape and contours of a mountain; be sure to have crevasses.
5. Mix a paste of water and wheat paste flour according to package directions.
6. Soak strips of newspaper in the wheat paste mixture.
7. Slap these messy strips onto the newspaper/oatmeal container mountain.
8. Repeat until all is covered with at least two layers of paste-soaked newspaper strips.
9. Let this structure dry for several days, then repeat the process using paper towel strips soaked in the paste mixture.
10. Using your hands, apply a coat of the wheat paste mixture to smooth out all the little tags of paper.
11. Allow this structure to dry.
12. When it is thoroughly dry, paint it with shades of green, brown, and gray to make it look natural. Now it is ready to add to a model railroad layout.

LANGUAGE ARTS ACTIVITY

▪ *Railroad Songs*

Railroading spurs us on to singing. Perhaps it is the rhythm of wheels upon the track, clickity-clack. Have your group members search for and collect railroad songs, for example, "New River Train," an early American song. Select a few to learn well. Present these at a concert after the group's model train and layout have been assembled.

POEM

Westcott, Nadine Bernard, illustrator. *I've Been Working on the Railroad*. Hyperion Books for Children, 1996.

VOCABULARY GROWTH WORDS

Benchwork: The structure upon which the model railroad is built; often it is constructed of 4-by-8-inch plywood attached to sawhorses.

Gauge: Gauges common to model railroading are: G, 1.77 inches between the rails; O, 1.26 inches; S, .87 inch; and HO, .66 inch.

Layout: The term given to the model railroad display in its entirety.

Power pack: An electrical device to reduce household electricity voltage and to convert it to direct current.

Prototype: The full-size train upon which the construction of the model train is based.

Restoration: A model train that has been restored to its original condition.

Roadbed: The material upon which the track is laid. In model railroading layouts it may be cork.

Scale: The proportion or ratio that compares the size of the model railroad to the size of a real train.

Scale model railroaders: People who are enthusiastic about creating scale models of trains.

Swap meet: An event during which hobbyists can buy or sell paraphernalia.

Transformer: An electrical device that converts 110 voltages to lower current to run model trains.

RESOURCES

National Model Railroad Association, Inc.
4121 Cromwell Road
Chattanooga, TN 37421-2119
http://www.nmra.org

Originally based out of Milwaukee, Wisconsin, NMRA is "the largest organization devoted to the development, promotion, and enjoyment of the hobby of model railroading." The extensive Web site provides information about conventions, educational programs, and publications.

READ MORE ABOUT IT

Grams, John. *Toy Train Collecting and Operating: An Introduction to the Hobby.* Kalmbach, 1999. 112p. (I–A)

Written primarily for toy train collectors, this book also provides a good introduction to setting up a model railroad layout. How to re-create a layout, make scenery, lay down track, and install the roadbed are all sections that the young hobbyist will be able to use; older readers will find the information on collecting and displaying collectible toy trains valuable. The last sections of the book contain the names and addresses of associations and manufacturers as well as a list of related books. Interesting facts are scattered throughout the text including a socioeconomic breakdown of the adult toy track collector. These folks became interested in this hobby when they were children and renewed their interest when they were in their 30s. Model railroad hobbyists can count Frank Sinatra among their members. A picture of his toy train collection appears in the book.

Griffiths, Rose. *Railroads.* Gareth Stevens, 1995. 32p. Photographs by Peter Millard. (P)

This is no ordinary book about railroads. It twists play with model railroads into math lessons for the young. What a creative way to think! Simple text poses problem-solving questions to children as they play with their model railroad. Peter Millard's bright photographs attract the reader into the action. Although this book, part of the First Step Math series, is found in the math section, it contains a model railroad glossary and resources.

Press, Judy. *Vroom! Vroom!: Making 'Dozers, 'Copters, Trucks & More.* Williamson, 1997. 160p. Illustrated by Michael Kline. (P–I)

This book isn't exclusively about model trains, but it does have clever ideas for items that could be used in a model railroad layout. Directions are given for constructing light signals, tunnels, and bridges as well as model trucks, cars, helicopters, and boats. Vroom! vroom! your way to fun with children.

Townsley, John. *Getting Started with Model Trains*. Sterling, 1991. 96p. (I)

Black-and-white photographs generously distributed throughout this book make clear the major points and how-tos of model railroading. The hobby of model trains has been around for 150 years and continues to grow. The hands-on experience continues to fascinate young children. This comprehensive resource book provides names and addresses of manufacturers and suppliers, and estimates of the cost of a tabletop layout. Computers and video have changed this hobby. Enthusiasts may now use software to design the layout and a miniature video camera to project the scenery from the engineer's perspective.

Young, Caroline, and Colin King. *Railways and Trains*. Usborne, 1991. 48p. (P–I)

Young and King recount the history of trains and railways. They tell how railways were built; the story of early competition among early locomotive engineers, and the subsequent improvements in locomotives and railways. The information in the book will provide hobbyists with background information that will help them understand their hobby even more.

30 WEAVING

Weaving joins together beauty with manual dexterity to produce a satisfying, useful, or decorative article. As young weavers ply their hobby, they are using the following skills: color sense, design, fine muscle coordination, dexterity, hand-eye coordination, spatial relations, and mathematics. The opportunities for studying weaving designs, looms, and techniques of many cultures and ethnic groups are numerous and varied.

Possible careers that result from an early interest in weaving include interior decorator, fabric designer, textile researcher, folk art researcher, curator, professional weaver, teacher, and computer program designer.

London, Jonathan. *The Village Basket Weaver*. Dutton Children's Books, 1996. Unpaged. Illustrated by George Crespo. (P)

Carefully researched by both author and illustrator, this story recounts the passing on of the tradition of weaving cassava baskets from grandfather to grandson. This intergenerational story is set in a Carib Town in Belize where cassava is a mainstay of the native diet. It is critical to the welfare of the village that someone learns the basket weaving craft. Tavio, the grandson, meets the challenge and learns his grandfather's craft. Crespo's illustrations add authenticity to the story.

HOBBY STARTER ACTIVITY

▪ *Mug Mat*

This activity should be broken into several sessions. To ask a child to sit in one spot for an hour wiggling a needle over and under warp cords may be unrealistic. But for 7 to 10 minutes at a time, it would be fun.

Yarn choice is another critical factor in this project's success. An assortment of brightly colored thick yarns works well.

The child's developmental stage is important also. A 10-year-old with fine motor coordination under control will be happier with weaving than a seven-year-old still struggling with shoelace tying.

Materials

Clean Styrofoam meat trays or stiff cardboard (approximately 4½" x 8")

Scissors

Combs (one per child)

Large-eyed needles (These are labeled "children's needles"—Wright's #7508.)

Strong, non-stretchable cord or string. Carpet warp is ideal but cotton string will do. 166" per tray.

Brightly colored yarn cut into 30" lengths

Cocoa in mugs for the last day celebration

Audiotapes or CDs of children's music

Preparation

Everyone will be happier to do this project if you and a few friends prepare the looms. It will probably take about 15 minutes per loom. You will need one Styrofoam tray, 166 inches of warping thread per loom, a large-eyed needle, and scissors.

1. Cut 10 ¼-inch slits at both the top and bottom of the tray. Be sure that the slits are about ¼ inch apart.
2. Thread the needle with the warping cord. Make a knot at one end of the cord.
3. Warp the loom. Start at the right-hand bottom corner of the Styrofoam tray. Slip the knot behind that first slit. Bring the warping thread to the front of the tray.
4. Wind the warping thread up the front of the tray, through the slit at the top around the back, and up through the second slit at the bottom. Keep on in this manner making parallel, evenly spaced windings. Keep the tension even.
5. Secure the end of the warping cord with a knot that is drawn snug against the tray. To be sure that the warp stays tight, place strips of transparent tape across the warping cords at the back of the tray.

6. Secure the top and bottom of the warp with a row or two of chain stitches. This is a very important step because it spaces the warp cords and keeps the warp even and under even tension.
7. To start the chain stitch, thread a needle with a strand of the warping cord. Then tie a knot on the lower right-hand warp cord.
8. Follow the pattern shown for the chain stitch in Figure 30.1. Chain stitch one or two rows at the top and bottom of the warp. This step begins the weft, which is the set of cross threads of weaving.

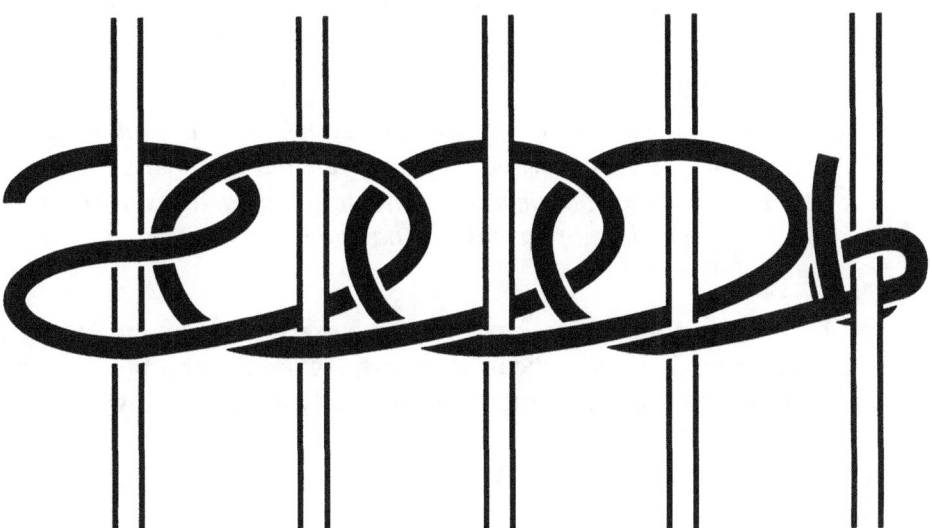

Figure 30.1. Chain stitch.

9. Keep the weft loose. Do not allow the edges of the warp to pull in. Keep the warp in line. You are ready to demonstrate how to weave to your group.

Weaving

Distribute the prepared looms, strands of yarn, needles, and combs to each child. Say to your group:

> *During the next few minutes, we are going to learn how to do needle weaving. Here are a few things you need to keep in mind as we weave.*
>
> *1. When you weave, you move the needle and thread in an over and under motion. Move the needle and thread over the first cord of the warp and under the next cord (demonstrate). So remember: over, under,*

> *over, under. When you weave the next row, do the opposite: under, over, under, over.*
>
> 2. *Don't pull the weft strand tight. The weft is the set of cross threads in a weaving. Keep the weft loose. Watch the sides. Don't let the sides pull in at all. Keep the warp cords even and parallel.*
>
> 3. *As you weave, lay the weft thread at a diagonal (demonstrate). This helps to keep the weft loose. With the comb (weavers call this a beater), push the diagonal weft into line and up against the row before it.*
>
> *Now we are ready to weave! Thread your needle and take the strand of yarn over and under the warp cords. Weave your mat in one color, in stripes, or in as many colors of yarn as we have here.*

Put on the music, have your group weave for up to 10 minutes, and then stop for the day. During the next session, when the children have finished weaving to the top row of chain stitch, you are ready to explain how to finish off the weaving.

Finishing

Say to the children:

> *Turn your loom over and cut across the warp halfway from the top and bottom. Take about two strands of warp cords and tie these with a loose overhand knot. Make the knot snug against the chain stitch edge. Continue knotting across the edge. Repeat at the other end. Cut this fringe to a desired length.*

Next, distribute mugs of cocoa. Tell the children what is good about each of their mug mats: straight edges, great color choice, interesting color combination, pretty stripe patterns, etc. Praise them thoroughly for creating something that didn't exist before.

LANGUAGE ARTS ACTIVITY

▪ *Weaving a Story Line*

Story writing is much like weaving. The plot is like the warp through which story embellishments and details are woven. The plot or story line sets the pattern. Plots have particular forms. Some are problem-centered, others follow a predictable plan based on a repeated sequence such as time, counting, or accumulation; some are episodic.

As a group, have the children use the following episodic pattern to create a patterned story line.

In the spring it is so _____.

We like to _____, _____, and _____.

We see _____, _____, and _____.

We _____, _____, and _____.
    (verb)   (verb)   (verb)

We feel _____.

In the spring it is so _____. (Repeat the pattern with summer, fall, and winter).

All round the year we _____, _____, _____, and _____.

POEM

Yuan, Chen. "Song of the Weaving Woman." In *Saturday's Children, Poems of Work* compiled by Helen Plotz. Greenwillow Books, 1982.

VOCABULARY GROWTH WORDS

Beater: The part of the loom that is moved back and forth to pack the weft rows into the warp.

Bobbin: A small spool wound with thread.

Harnesses: The frames that hold the heddles.

Heddles: The wire loops attached to heddle bars through which the warp threads pass.

Loom: The framework upon which the warp is stretched across and at a tension for weaving cloth.

Shed: The opening made between warp threads through which the shuttle may pass.

Shuttle: The wooden device around which the weaving thread is wound.

Tabby: Plain weave; a pattern in which the weft and warp threads are at right angles.

Tapestry: A technique for weaving in which the design threads of one part are interlocked with those in an adjacent part.

Warp: Those threads that are stretched lengthwise across the loom.

Weft: The crosswise threads used in weaving cloth.

RESOURCES

Handweavers Guild of America, Inc.
3327 Duluth Highway Suite 20
Duluth, GA 30196-3301
http://www.weavespindye.org

HGA encourages and supports the fiber arts—including dyeing, spinning, and weaving—through educational and certification programs. The Web site provides information about their members-only independent study program; scholarships for students pursuing degrees in the field of fiber arts; and conferences, events, and competitions. The Web site includes a FAQ page and links to related organizations and guilds.

READ MORE ABOUT IT

Fisher, Leonard Everett. *The Weavers*. Benchmark Books, 1998. 45p. (I)
 Colonial America is the setting for award-winning author Leonard Fisher's historical look at weaving. Fisher describes in detail weaving techniques, tools, and patterns. His precise draftsman-like drawings enhance the book. A glossary is included.

Lasky, Kathryn. *The Weaver's Gift*. Warne, 1980. Unpaged. Photographs by Christopher G. Knight. (I)
 In this recounting, Carolyn, a weaver who raises her own sheep for the wool, follows all the steps necessary to go from sheep to baby blanket over many months. After the sheep are shorn, Max, the toddler from next door, helps Carolyn prepare the fleece for spinning. In the fall, after she selects herbs for dyeing the fiber and dresses her loom, Carolyn weaves the blanket that she had planned. Max helps her. To Max's great delight Carolyn decides to give the blanket to him. The black-and-white photographs clarify the detailed text and capture the joy as well as the hard work of the weaver.

O'Reilly, Susie. *Weaving*. Thomson Learning, 1993. 32p. Illustrated by Zul Mukhida. (P–I)

O'Reilly, an experienced author of arts and crafts books, has written another of value for the young crafter. She explains in clear, easy-to-follow directions how to construct a warp and how to weave a variety of projects. She includes directions for weaving with paper and for weaving an ikat project.

Sola, Michelle. *Angela Weaves a Dream: The Story of a Young Maya Artist*. Hyperion Books for Children, 1994. 48p. Photographs by Jeffrey Jay Foxx. (I)

The seven sacred Mayan weaving patterns and the stories behind them are woven into this photo essay. Angela, a beginning weaver, hopes to win the First Sampler prize to be awarded to the best first weaving. Step by step, the reader is guided from carding wool to dyeing to learning to use the backstrap loom, which are described as Angela learns to weave and listens to the ancient stories from Abuelita.

Wiseman, Ann Sayre. *Making Things: The Handbook of Creative Discovery*. Little, Brown, 1997. 176p. (I)

Pages 86 to 101 of this valuable book describe various weaving techniques and weaving-related projects. Children will learn twisting, twining, thrumming, as well as weaving by using patterns. Various types of looms and the instructions for making them are given: thrumming loom, inkle loom, Popsicle stick heddle loom, and plastic drinking straw belt loom are a few. This book, written over many years, by Ann Wiseman, a former program director at Boston Children's Museum is a compilation of Wiseman's activity directions used at the museum. With more than 100 activities and their instructions clearly written, a child will never have to whine, "I have nothing to do." With a modicum of adult encouragement and support, children will be both educated and entertained.

ACTIVITIES INDEX

Hobby Starter Activities

Adopt a Horse, 43
Adopt a Kitty, Share a Cat, 14
Begin Your Stamp Collection, 112
Bird Feeders, 8
Build a Castle, Build Your Vocabulary, 2
Celebrate Working Dogs—National Dog Week September 19–25, 22
Construct a Handbell, 72
Create an Egg Tree, 32
Crystal Growing, 96
Face Painting, 36
Fantasy Masks, 66
Garbage Bag Kites, 60
Going on a Bug Hunt, 48
Greenware Pottery, 76
Have a Neighborhood Game Festival, 84
Have Mini Flannel Board, Will Travel, 128
Insect Zoo, 47
It's 5/25! Time to Jig and Jive! (National Tap Dance Day), 18
Make a Memory Scrapbook, 102
Make a Toy Contest, 142
More They Draw, the Better They Draw, The, 28
Mug Mat, 154
Neighborhood Vaudeville and Talent Show, 108
Oatmeal Container Tunnel and Mountain, 148
Puppet Stage, 80
Quilt Patch, 90
Stargazers' Club, 116
Taffy Pull, 120
Terry Cloth Teddy Bear, 136
Zipper Pull, 54

Language Arts Activities

Architect's Sketchbook, 3
Art Talks, 28
Audience Participation Story, 131
Chart, dog name, 23
Children Have Always Wanted to Have Fun: A Research Project, 143
Creating a Business Plan, 121
Dancing Poetry Bulletin Board, A, 18
Demonstration Speech, 55
Diamante, 9
Dog Name Chart, 23
Egg Tree Show and Tell, 32
Favorite Familiar Folktale Script, 80
Feline Photos, 14
Fish Sandwich Books, 40
I-Shaped Paragraphs, 49
Listening to a Guest Speaker, 112
Little Theater, A, 67
"Mail-Order" Catalog, 76
Master/Apprentice Fishing School, 39
Petroglyphs and the Sidewalk Chalk Connection, 97
Plays Starring Stars, 116
Quilting Bee Discussion, 91
Railroad Songs, 149
Scrapbook Captions, 103
Show Biz Posters, 108
Survey, 44
Syncopated Silliness, 72
Teddy Bear Celebration, 138
Two-Column Dialogue, 36
Videotape: You Learned It, Now Teach It, 62
Weaving a Story Line, 157
Word Games, 85

Activities Resources

ABC Quilts, 92
Amateur Entomologists' Society Bug Club, 50
American Architectural Foundation, 4
American Association of Amateur Astronomers, 117
American Cat Fanciers Association, 15
American Jigsaw Puzzle Society, 87
American Kennel Club, 24
American Kitefliers Association, 63
American Philatelic Society, 113
American Quilter's Society, 92
Audubon Society. *See* National Audubon Society
Bass Anglers Sportsman Society, 40
Bead Museum, 56
Children's Music Network, 73
Crayola.com, 29
Good Bears of the World, 139
Guide Dogs for the Blind, 24
Handweavers Guild of America, 158
International Brotherhood of Magicians, 109
International Clown Hall of Fame, 37
International Jugglers Association, 109
International Top Spinners Association, 144
J. B. Speed Art Museum, 4
Jangle.com Scrapbooking and Memory Crafts, 104
Junior Achievement International, 123
Junior Philatelists of America, 113
Kids 'N' Clay Pottery Studio, 77
Masks.org, 68
Mineralogical Society of America, 98
National Audubon Society, 10
National Dance Association, 19
National Model Railroad Association, 150
National Wildlife Federation, 10
Puppeteers of America, 81
Pysanka by Adriana, 33
Scrapbooking.com, 104
Storytelling Foundation International, 132
United States Pony Clubs, 45

AUTHOR/TITLE/SUBJECT INDEX

Ackerman, Karen, 107
Adventures in Art (Milord), 29
Ahlberg, Allen, 111
Ahlberg, Janet, 111
Alborough, Jez, 135
All About Pattern, 30
Allen, Jody, 113
Amazing Egg Book, The (Griffin and Seed), 33
American Quilt-Making: Stories in Cloth (Stalcup), 93
Ancona, George, 19
Angela Weaves a Dream: The Story of a Young Maza Artist (Sola), 159
Architecture (Pratt), 5
Architecture (Wood), 5
Ardley, Neil, 74
Arnosky, Jim, 41
Arnsteen, Katy Keck, 110
Art Lesson, The (dePaola), 27
Asimov, Isaac, 117

Backyard Birds (Pine), 11
Baker Baker Cookie Maker (Hayward), 79
Balit, Christina, 118
Barber, Antonia, 13
Bayley, Nicola, 13
Beading (Sadler), 57
Becoming Your Cat's Best Friend (Gutman), 15
Ben's Trumpet (Isadora), 71
Bentley, Nancy, 110
Bial, Raymond, 92
Big Bear's Book (Bjork), 139
Big Book of Games, The (Stott), 88
Big Bug Book, The (Facklam), 51
Big Tales from Near to Far (Milord), 12
Bird Talk (Jonas), 11
Birds (Ricciuti), 11
Biz Kids' Guide to Success: Money-Making Ideas for Young Entrepreneurs (Thompson), 124
Bjork, Christina, 139

Bolick, Nancy O'Keefe, 113
Bowling Alone (Putnam), xi
Braren, Loretta Trezzo, 74
Brannon, Tom, 79
Briekman, David F., 83
Briggs, Michael, 114
Brock, Barbara, x
Brown, Caleb, 72
Brown, Marc, 119
Brown, Margaret Wise, 147
Bruchac, Joseph, 132
Brumbeau, Jeff, 89
Build Your Own Castle (Petty), 2

Caldecott, Barrie, 63
Call! The History of the U.S. Mail Service (Bolick), 113
Calmenson, Stephanie, 87
Campbell, Annie, 133
Caney, Steven, 144
Castles, 2
Catch the Wind: All About Kites (Gibbons), 63
Cathedral Mouse (Chorao), 1
Cats: From Tigers to Tabbies (Higgins), 15
Children's Poetry Index, xiii
Choosing the Perfect Cat (Kelsey-Wood), 16
Clowning Around (Falwell), 35
Cobb, Mary, 92
Cohen, Miriam, 65
Cole, Joanna, 15, 87
Colon, Raul, 17
Color (Heller), 29
Companion Dogs: More Than Best Friends (Ring), 25
Constellations (Sipiera and Sipiera), 118
Couter, Robert B., xvi
Crazy Eights and Other Card Games (Cole and Calmenson), 87
Crinkleroot's 24 Fish Every Child Should Know (Arnosky), 41

Crystals and Crystal Gardens You can Grow (Stangl), 99
Cummings, Pat, 133

Dance (Grau), 19
Dance (Tythacott), 20
deBeer, Sara, 74
Decorating Eggs (Pollak), 34
DeMarcken, Gail, 89
dePaola, Tomie, 27
Diehn, Owen, 104
Dogs (Gibbons), 25
Dog Training Projects for Young People (McMains), 25
Doney, Meryl, 56, 68, 144
Doty, Roy, 145
Dragonflies (Merrick), 51
Drew, Helen, 74
Dugan, Barbara, 141

Edin, Peter, 110
Editors of Klutz Press, 38, 87
Eggs Beautiful: How to Make Ukrainian Easter Eggs (Luciow, Kmit, and Luciow), 34
Egg Tree, The (Milhous), 31
Ehlert, Lois, 7
Ellis, Jan Davey, 92
Engel, Diana, 75
Erlbach, Arlene, 124, 139

Face Painting (Editors of Klutz Press), 38
Face Painting (Lincoln), 38
Face Painting (Russon), 38
Facklam, Margery, 51
Facklam, Paul, 51
Falwell, Cathryn, 35
Family Scrapbook Paper Pizazz (McNeill and Stiles), 104
Fancher, Lou, 47
Feathers for Lunch (Ehlert), 11
Feature Analysis, xvi–xvii
Feeding Our Feathered Friends (Spaulding), 11
Fired Up: Making Pottery in Ancient Time (Gonen), 78
First Look at Rocks, A (Selsam and Hunt), 99
Fish in a Flash (Arnosky), 41
Fisher, Leonard Everett, 158
Fishing (Whieldon), 41
Flanagan, Alice, 68

Florian, Douglas, 77
Flying Toys (Milner), 63
Follow the Stars: A Native American Woodlands Tale (Rodanas), 115
Ford, Harry, 117
Foxx, Jeffrey Jay, 159
Friendly Guide to the Universe: A Down-to-Earth Tour of Space, Time and the Wonders of the Cosmos, The (Hathaway), 117
Fun on the Run: Travel Games and Songs (Cote and Samuelson), 87
Fun with Modeling Clay (Reid), 78

Gallery of Games, A (Marchon-Arnaud), 87
Gammell, Stephen, 107
Garcia, Jerry, 140
Garden Birds of America (Harrison), 11
Gayle, Katie, 56
Gelber, Carol, 68
Getting Started in Stamp Collecting (Hobson), 114
Getting Started with Model Trains (Townsley), 151
Gibbons, Gail, 4, 25, 63, 78
Gizmos and Gadgets: Creating Science Contraptions That Work and Knowing Why (Hanson), 144
Gold! The True Story of Why People Search for It, Mine It, Trade It, Steal It, Mint It, Hoard It, Shape It, Wear It, Fight and Kill for It (Meltzer), 99
Gonen, Rivka, 78
Gordon, Maria, 98
Gordon, Mike, 98
Granger, Neill, 114
Grau, Andree, 19
Gray, Libba Moore, 17
Great Kite Book, The (Schmidt), 64
Green, Anne Canevari, 15
Greene, Graham, iv
Griffin, Barbara Budge, 132
Griffin, Margaret, 33
Grisman, David, 140
Gutherie, Donna, 110
Gutman, Bill, 15

Hague, Michael, 34
Halperin, Wendy Anderson, 124
Hamanaka, Sheila, 19
Harper, Peter, 110
Harrison, George, 11
Hamilton, Martha, 133
Hart, Avery, 2, 20, 74

Hathaway, Nancy, 117
Hauser, Jill Frankel, 144
Hayward, Linda, 79
Heller, Ruth, 29
Henson, Cheryl, 82
Heyman, Ken, 139
Higgins, Maria Mihalik, 15
Hoban, Lillian, 65
Hobson, Burton, 114
Hokey Pokey, The (Hamanaka), 19
Hold Your Horses: A Feedbag Full of Fact and Fable (Meltzer), 45
Hoofbeats: The Story of a Thoroughbred (McFarland), 45
Horsepower: The Wonder of Draft Horses (Peterson), 46
Houses (Venturo), 5
Houses of China (Shemie), 5
How a House Is Built (Gibbons), 4
How Teddy Bears Are Made: A Visit to the Vermont Teddy Bear Factory (Morris), 139
Hunt, Joyce, 99

I Can Make Toys (Wallace), 144
I Didn't Know That Some Bugs Glow in the Dark (Llewellyn), 51
In the Easter Basket (Sechrist), 34
Incredible Fishing Stories (Morey), 41
Isadora, Rachel, 71
It's the Bear (Alborough), 135
Ivory, Lesley Anne, 16

Jackman, Joan, 110
Jenkins, Martin, 51
Jewelry (Doney), 56
Jewelry (Robson), 56
Jewelry (Tythacott), 57
Johnson, Dale, xvi
Jolly Postman, The (Ahlberg and Ahlberg), 111
Jonas, Ann, 11
Juba This and Juba That (Tashjian), 133

Keegan, Shannon, 124
Kelsey-Wood, Dennis, 16
Kelsey-Wood, Eve, 16
Key Art Terms for Beginners (Yenawine), 30
Kids Best Dog Book (Rosen), 25
Kid's Book of Fishing, The (Rosen), 41

Kids' Business Book (Erlbach), 124
Kid's Guide to Money, The (Otfinoski), 124
Kids Make Music (Hart and Mantell), 20, 74
Kids Travel (Editors of Klutz Press), 87
King, Colin, 151
Kites (Caldecott), 63
Kline, Michael, 144, 150
Kmit, Ann, 34
Knight, Christopher G., 158
Knights and Castles, 2
Koelsch, Michael, 74
Kohl, Mary Ann, 78

Lade, Roger, 82
Lasky, Kathryn, 158
Lee, Dennis, 3
Let's Dance! (Anacona), 19
Lewin, Ted, 127
Littlechild, George, 43
Little Lump of Clay, The (Engel), 75
Little Pigs Puppet Book, The (Watson), 82
Llewellyn, Claire, 51
London, Jonathon, 153
Loo-Loo, Boo and Art You Can Do (Rocke), 30
Loop the Loop (Dugan), 141
Luciow, Johanna, 34
Luciow, Loretta, 34
Luenn, Nancy, 39
Lyons, Mary, 93

MacDonald, Margaret Read, 131, 133
Makeup Art (Truman), 37
Making Books (Stowell), 105
Making Books That Fly, Fold, Wrap, Hide, Pop-up, Twist and Turn: Books for Kids to Make (Diehn), 104
Making Kites (Michael), 63
Making Masks (McNiven and McNiven), 69
Making Music: 6 Instruments You Can Create (Oates), 74
Making Scrapbooks: Complete Guide to Preserving Your Treasured Memories (Vanessa-Ann), 105
Making Things: The Handbook of Creative Discovery (Wiseman), 159
Mantell, Paul, 2, 20
Marchon-Arnaud, Catherine, 87
Marzollo, Jean, 140
Masks (Doney), 68
Masks! (Flanagan), 68

Masks (Wright), 69
Masks Tell Stories (Gelber), 68
Mayer, Mercer, 59
McCurdy, Michael, 93
McFarland, Cynthia, 45
McKay, Griffin, 132
McMains, Joel M., 25
McMeel, Andrew, 104
McNeill, Suzanne, 104
McNiven, Helen, 69, 82
McNiven, Peter, 69, 82
Meet My Cats (Ivory), 16
Meltzer, Milton, 45, 99
Merrick, Patrick, 51
Michael, David, 63
Michael Hague's Family Easter Treasury (Hague), 34
Milhous, Katherine, 31
Millard, Peter, 150
Miller, Margaret, 15
Milner, Sally, 63
Milord, Susan, 12, 29
Mitchelson, Mitch, 110
Mitton, Jacqueline, 118
Moller, Ray, 110
Moments to Remember: The Art of Creating Scrapbook Mail Memories (Packham), 104
Monarch Magic (Rosenblatt), 51
Moneymakers: Good Cents for Girls (Roper), 125
Morey, Shaun, 41
Morgan, Mary, 25
Morris, Ann, 139
Most Excellent Book of How To Be a Clown, The (Perkins and Roden), 110
Most Excellent Book of How To Be a Juggler, The (Mitchelson), 110
Most Excellent Book of How To Be a Magician, The (Edin), 110
Most Excellent Book of How To Be a Puppeteer, The (Lade), 82
Mousehole Cat, The (Barber), 13
Mudworks (Nohl), 78
Mukhida, Zul, 159
Multicultural applications, 5, 12, 17, 19, 20, 31, 35, 53, 56, 57, 59, 63, 65, 68, 71, 74, 75, 78, 79, 93, 114, 115, 127, 141, 144, 153
Music (Ardley), 74
Munoz, William, 45
Muppets Make Puppets (Henson), 82
My Fellow Americans: A Family Album (Provensen), 101
My First Music Book (Drew), 74

My First Paint Book (Sirett), 30
My Life in Dog Years (Paulsen), 25
My Mama Had a Dancing Heart (Gray), 17
My New Kitten (Cole), 15
My Pony Book (Pritchard), 46

National TV Turnoff Week, x
Nessa's Fish (Luenn), 39

Oates, Eddie Herschel, 74
Officer Buckle and Gloria (Rathmann), 21
Once Upon a Company: A True Story (Halperin), 124
Open Ears: Music Adventures for a New Generation (deBeer), 74
O'Reilly, Susie, 159
Ornithology, 7
Otfinski, Steve, 124
Otto, Carolyn, 25
Our Puppies Are Growing (Otto), 25

Packham, Jo, 104
Patent, Dorothy Hinshaw, 45
Paul, Ann Whitford, 93
Paulsen, Gary, 25
Pearson, P. David, xvi
Perkins, Catherine, 110
Peterson, Cris, 46
Peterson First Grade to Rocks and Minerals (Pough), 99
Petty, Nate, 2
Pickin' Peas (MacDonald), 131, 133
Pine, Jonathan, 11
Polka Bats and Octopus Slacks (Brown), 72
Pollak, Jane, 34
Potter, A (Florian), 77
Pottery Place, The (Gibbons), 78
Pough, Frederick H., 99
Pratt, Paula Bryant, 5
Press, Judy, 150
Pritchard, Louise, 46
Provensen, Alice, 101
Puppets (McNiven and McNiven), 82
Puppets (Wright), 82
Putnam, Robert, xi
Putting on a Play: The Young Playwright's Guide to Scripting, Directing, and Performing (Bentley and Gutherie), 110

Quarter Horses (Hinshaw), 45
Quest for the One Big Thing, The (Fancher), 47
Quilt-Block History of Pioneer Days with Projects Kids Can Make (Cobb), 9
Quilt Maker's Gift (Brumbeau), 89
Quilts from Caring Hands, xi

Railroads (Griffiths), 150
Railways and Trains (Young and King), 151
Rathmann, Peggy, 21
Real-Skin Rubber Monster Mask, The (Cohen), 65
Reid, Barbara, 78
Reid, Margarette, 53
Reutzel, D. Ray, xiv
Ricciuti, Edward, 11
Ring, Elizabeth, 25
Ringgold, Faith, 90
Robins, Jim, 105
Robson, Denny, 56
Rock Instrumental Classics, 72
Rocke, Denis M., 30
Rocks and Soil (Gordon), 98
Rodanas, Kristina, 115
Roden, Katie, 110
Roosevelt, Franklin Delano, x
Roper, Ingrid, 125
Rosen, Michael J., 25, 41
Rosenblatt, Lynn, 51

Sadler, Judy Ann, 57
Sams, Kenneth, 63
Sans Souci, Daniel, 83
Schmidt, Norman, 64
Schweninger, Ann, 140
Seasons Sewn, The (Paul), 93
Sechrisl, Elizabeth Hough, 34
Seed, Deborah, 33
Seiden, Art, 147
Selsam, Millicent, 99
Semantic Webbing, xvi
Shemie, Bonnie, 5
Shibumi and the Kitemaker (Mayer), 59
Shone, Rob, 82, 110
Sinatra, Frank, x
Sipiera, Diane M., 118
Sipiera, Paul P., 118
Sirett, Dawn, 30
Snappy, Jazzy Jewelry (Gayle), 56
Sola, Michelle, 159
Song and Dance Man (Ackerman), 107

Space Sputter's Guide, The (Asimov), 117
Spaulding, Dean T., 11
Springer, Harriett, 99
Stalcup, Ann, 34, 93
Stamp Collecting (Granger), 114
Stamps (Briggs), 114
Stangl, Jean, 99
Steig, William, 95
Steven Caney's Toy Book (Caney), 144
Stevens, Gareth, 117
Stevenson, James, 141
Stitching Stars: The Story Quilts of Harriet Powers (Lyons), 93
Stites, Lani, 104
Stories in My Pocket (Hamilton and Weiss), 133
Storyteller's Handbook (Griffin), 132
Storytellers, The (Lewin), 127
Stott, Dorothy, 88
Stowell, Charlotte, 105
String of Beads, A (Reid), 53
Sylvester and the Magic Pebble (Steig), 95
Synarski, Susan, 125

Tar Beach, 90
Tashjian, Virginia, 133
Teaching Children to Read (Reutzel and Couter), xiv
Teaching Reading Vocabulary (Johnson and Pearson), xvi
Teddy Bear Book, The (Marzollo), 140
Teddy Bears (Erlbach), 139
Teddy Bear's Picnic (Garcia and Grisman), 140
Tell Me a Tale (Bruchac), 132
Thompson, Terri, 124
Three Dimensional Medieval Castle, A, 2
Tiegreen, Alan, 87
Tong, Willabel, 2
Tops: Building and Experimenting with Spinning Toys (Zubrowski), 145
Townsley, John, 151
Toys (Doney), 144
Train to Timbuctoo, The (Brown), 147
Truman, Ron, 37
Tythacott, Louise, 20, 57

Ukrainian Egg Decoration: A Holiday Tradition (Stalcup), 34
Upitis, Alvis, 46
Usborne Guide to Stamps and Stamp Collecting (Allen), 113

Van Camp, Richard, 43
Vanessa-Ann, 105
Venn Diagram, xvii–xviii
Venturo, Piero, 5
Village Weaver, The (London), 153
Vroom! Vroom! Making 'Dozers, 'Copters, Trucks & More (Press), 150

Waldman, Neil, 39
Walker, Tracy, 57
Wallace, Mary, 144
Watson, N. Cameron, 82
Weavers, The (Fisher), 158
Weaver's Gift, The (Lasky), 15
Weaving (O'Reilly), 159
Weiss, Mitch, 133
Westcott, Nadine Bernard, 133
Whately, Bruce, 140
What's the Most Beautiful Thing You Know About Horses? (Van Camp), 43

Whieldon, Tony, 41
Winfrey, Oprah, x
Wingertu, Linda S., 12
Wings, Stings, and Wriggly Things (Jenkins), 51
Wiseman, Ann Sayre, 159
With Needle and Thread (Bial), 92
Wood, Richard, 5
Wright, Lyndie, 69, 82

Yates, Irene, 30
Yenawine, Philip, 30
Young Astronomer, The (Ford), 110
Young, Caroline, 151
Young Gymnast, The (Jackman), 110

Zickefoose, Julie, 11
Zoo in the Sky: A Book of Animal Constellations (Milton), 118
Zubrowski, Bernie, 145

ABOUT THE AUTHOR

Born and raised in rural Pennsylvania, Nancy Allen Jurenka enjoyed exploring the natural wonders of that area. Identifying birds, poking around limestone caves, wading in Conocochegue Creek to find tadpoles, collecting rocks—all were ways to enjoy a Pennsylvania summer afternoon. At night there was stargazing and insect collecting. Adults who had hobbies and professions shared their expertise with her. Mr. Highberger, a family friend, was an architect who shared his knowledge about building design, as well as his passion for stamp collecting. Mr. MacClay, her next door neighbor, taught her how to thread a worm onto a fishhook. Watching the enthusiasm of the teens in her father's youth group as they pulled taffy in the family kitchen impressed her with the power of candy-making to bring a group together. When Nancy said, "Hey! Let's put on a play," she and her friends—Bobby, Linda, and Bev—found guidance from Mame Schlicter, another neighbor, as they put on *Tom Sawyer*. Nancy was surrounded by adults who saw that it was their responsibility to bring a child along.

Dr. Jurenka graduated from Wilson College and Indiana University. She teaches reading education and children's literature at Central Washington University in Ellensburg, Washington.

from *Teacher Ideas Press*

Top Books for Elementary Schools

GLUES, BREWS, AND GOOS
Recipes and Formulas for Almost Any Classroom Project
Diana F. Marks

You've got to have it! This indispensable activity book pulls together hundreds of practical, easy recipes and formulas for classroom projects. From paints and salt map mixtures to volcanic action formulas, these kid-tested projects make learning authentic and enjoyable. All projects use ingredients that are easy to find and processes that are up-to-date. **Grades K–6.**
xvi, 179p. 8½x11 paper ISBN 1-56308-362-0

SCIENCE THROUGH CHILDREN'S LITERATURE, 2d Edition
Carol M. Butzow and John W. Butzow

The Butzows' groundbreaking, critically acclaimed, and best-selling resource has been thoroughly revised and updated with new titles and new activities for today's classroom. More than 30 exciting instructional units integrate all areas of the curriculum and serve as models to educators at all levels. Adopted as a supplementary text in schools of education nationwide, this resource features outstanding children's fiction books that are rich in scientific concepts yet equally well known for their strong story lines and universal appeal. **Grades K–3.**
xix, 205p. 8½x11 paper ISBN 1-56308-651-4

MULTICULTURAL FOLKTALES
Readers Theatre for Elementary Students
Suzanne I. Barchers

Introduce your students to other countries and cultures through these engaging readers theatre scripts based upon traditional folk and fairy tales. Representing more than 30 countries and regions, the 40 reproducible scripts are accompanied by presentation suggestions and recommendations for props and delivery. **Grades 1–5.**
xxi, 188p. 8½x11 paper ISBN 1-56308-760-X

SUPER SIMPLE STORYTELLING
A Can-Do Guide for Every Classroom, Every Day
Kendall Haven

Aside from guides to more than 40 powerful storytelling exercises, you'll find the Golden List of what an audience really needs from storytelling, a proven, step-by-step system for successfully learning and remembering a story, and the Great-Amazing-Never-Fail Safety Net to prevent storytelling disasters. This system has been successfully used by more than 15,000 educators across the country. **All Levels.**
xxvii, 229p. 8½x11 paper ISBN 1-56308-681-6

MORE SOCIAL STUDIES THROUGH CHILDREN'S LITERATURE
An Integrated Approach
Anthony D. Fredericks

These dynamic literature-based activities will help you energize the social studies curriculum and implement national and state standards. Each of these 33 units offers book summaries, social studies topic areas, critical thinking questions, and dozens of easy-to-do activities for every grade level. The author also gives practical guidelines for integrating literature across the curriculum, lists of Web sites useful in social studies classes, and annotated bibliographies of related resources. **Grades K–5.**
xix, 225p. 8½x11 paper ISBN 1-56308-761-8

For a free catalog or to place an order, please contact:
Teacher Ideas Press • Dept. B050 • P.O. Box 6633 • Englewood, CO • 80155-6633
800-237-6124 • **www.lu.com/tip** • **Fax: 303-220-8843**

www.ingramcontent.com/pod-product-compliance
Lightning Source LLC
Chambersburg PA
CBHW080551230426
43663CB00015B/2788